# 2023 Quick Ninja Dual Zone Air Fryer Cookbook UK

**2000** Days Easy, Yummy and Crispy Recipes Book Air fryer Accessories for Beginners - Ready in Less Than 30 Min

*Sienna Whittaker*

Copyright© 2023 By Sienna Whittaker

**All rights reserved worldwide.**

No part of this book may be reproduced or transmitted in any form or by any means, electronic or mechanical, including photo- copying, recording or by any information storage and retrieval system, without written permission from the publisher, except for the inclusion of brief quotations in a review.

**Warning-Disclaimer**

The purpose of this book is to educate and entertain. The author or publisher does not guarantee that anyone following the techniques, suggestions, tips, ideas, or strategies will become successful. The author and publisher shall have neither liability or responsibility to anyone with respect to any loss or damage caused, or alleged to be caused, directly or indirectly by the information contained in this book.

# Table of Contents

Chapter 1     Breakfasts     / 4

Chapter 2     Family Favorites     / 12

Chapter 3     Fast and Easy Everyday Favourites     / 16

Chapter 4     Poultry     / 21

Chapter 5     Beef, Pork, and Lamb     / 30

Chapter 6     Fish and Seafood     / 38

Chapter 7     Snacks and Appetizers     / 46

Chapter 8     Vegetables and Sides     / 54

Chapter 9     Vegetarian Mains     / 62

Chapter 10     Desserts     / 66

Appendix :     Recipe Index     / 71

Its intuitive control panel and removable parts make it easy to use and maintain, allowing individuals to focus on the art of cooking without being burdened by complex technology.

## Useful Tips to Master Your Fryer

The Ninja Dual Fryer is a versatile kitchen appliance that provides a range of benefits to chefs and home cooks. However, mastering the use of this appliance requires an understanding of its unique features and functions. Here are some useful tips to help you master the Ninja Dual Fryer:

1. Familiarize yourself with the appliance's settings: The Ninja Dual Fryer features a range of cooking functions, including air fry, roast, reheat, and dehydrate. Familiarizing yourself with these settings will enable you to prepare a range of meals and ensure that your food is cooked to perfection.

2. Experiment with cooking times and temperatures: The Ninja Dual Fryer allows you to control the temperature and cooking time of your food, enabling you to adjust these settings according to your preference. Experimenting with different cooking times and temperatures will help you to discover the ideal settings for different types of food.

3. Use the two-drawer design to your advantage: The Ninja Dual Fryer's two-drawer design enables you to cook different types of food simultaneously, with separate temperature and time controls. You can take advantage of this feature by cooking different types of food together, reducing cooking time and increasing efficiency in the kitchen.

4. Use a cooking spray: While the Ninja Dual Fryer uses hot air technology to produce crispy and golden results with minimal oil usage, it is still advisable to use a cooking spray to ensure that your food does not stick to the drawer.

5. Clean the appliance regularly: The Ninja Dual Fryer is a user-friendly appliance that is easy to clean. Regular cleaning of the appliance's removable parts will ensure that it operates efficiently and maintains its optimal performance.

## Get to Cook Now

The Ninja Dual Fryer is an innovative kitchen appliance that provides a range of benefits to modern chefs and home cooks. Its unique features and functions, including hot air technology, two-drawer design, and diverse cooking functions, offer a healthier and more convenient alternative to traditional frying methods. By following the tips outlined above, individuals can master the use of this appliance and prepare delicious and healthy meals with ease and efficiency.

Therefore, we encourage readers to get cooking with their Ninja Dual Fryer, experiment with different settings, and discover the versatility and convenience this appliance has to offer. With the Ninja Dual Fryer, chefs and home cooks can elevate their culinary skills and create a range of delicious meals for themselves and their loved ones.

# Chapter 1   Breakfasts

## Potatoes Lyonnaise

### Prep time: 10 minutes | Cook time: 31 minutes | Serves 4

| | |
|---|---|
| 1 sweet/mild onion, sliced | thick |
| 1 teaspoon butter, melted | 1 tablespoon vegetable oil |
| 1 teaspoon soft brown sugar | Salt and freshly ground black |
| 2 large white potatoes (about | pepper, to taste |
| 450 g in total), sliced ½-inch | |

1. Toss the sliced onions, melted butter and soft brown sugar together in the air fryer drawer. Air fry for 8 minutes, shaking the drawer occasionally to help the onions cook evenly.
2. While the onions are cooking, bring a saucepan of salted water to a boil on the stove-top. Par-cook the potatoes in boiling water for 3 minutes. Drain the potatoes and pat them dry with a clean kitchen towel.
3. Add the potatoes to the onions in the air fryer drawer and drizzle with vegetable oil. Toss to coat the potatoes with the oil and season with salt and freshly ground black pepper.

Cook:
1. Set the air fryer to 200ºC.
2. Air fry for 20 minutes, tossing the vegetables a few times during the cooking time to help the potatoes brown evenly.
3. Season with salt and freshly ground black pepper and serve warm.

## Sausage Stuffed Peppers & Bacon Eggs on the Go

### Prep time: 20 minutes | Cook time: 15 minutes | Serves 2-4

**Sausage Stuffed Peppers**

| | |
|---|---|
| 230 g spicy pork sausage meat, removed from casings | drained |
| 4 large eggs | 4 green peppers |
| 110 g full-fat soft cheese, softened | 8 tablespoons grated chilli cheese |
| 60 g tinned diced tomatoes, | 120 ml full-fat sour cream |

**Bacon Eggs on the Go**

| | |
|---|---|
| 2 eggs | Salt and ground black |
| 110 g bacon, cooked | pepper, to taste |

Prepare for Sausage Stuffed Peppers
1. In a medium skillet over medium heat, crumble and brown the sausage meat until no pink remains. Remove sausage and drain the fat from the pan. Crack eggs into the pan, scramble, and cook until no longer runny.
2. Place cooked sausage in a large bowl and fold in soft cheese. Mix in diced tomatoes. Gently fold in eggs.
3. Cut a 4-inch to 5-inch slit in the top of each pepper, removing the seeds and white membrane with a small knife. Separate the filling into four servings and spoon carefully into each pepper. Top each with 2 tablespoons cheese.
4. Place each chili in Zone One of the air fryer.

Prepare for Bacon Eggs on the Go
1. Crack an egg into each of the cups and add the bacon. Season with some pepper and salt.
2. Put liners in a regular cupcake tin and place the paper cup in Zone Two of the air fryer.

Cook:
1. Select Zone Two and preheat the air fryer to 200ºC. Bake the Zone Two in the preheated air fryer for 15 minutes, or until the eggs are set.
2. Adjust the Zone One to 180ºC. Set the timer of Zone One for 15 minutes.
3. Press Start.
4. Make peppers in Zone One soft and cheese will be browned when ready. Serve warm and immediately with sour cream on top.

## Asparagus and Bell Pepper Strata

### Prep time: 10 minutes | Cook time: 14 to 20 minutes | Serves 4

| | |
|---|---|
| 8 large asparagus spears, trimmed and cut into 2-inch pieces | cut into ½-inch cubes |
| | 3 egg whites |
| 80 g grated carrot | 1 egg |
| 120 g chopped red pepper | 3 tablespoons 1% milk |
| 2 slices wholemeal bread, | ½ teaspoon dried thyme |

1. In a baking dish, combine the asparagus, carrot, red bell pepper, and 1 tablespoon of water into Zone One.
2. Add the bread cubes to the vegetables and gently toss.
3. In a medium bowl, whisk the egg whites, egg, milk, and thyme until frothy.
4. Pour the egg mixture into the pan of Zone Two.

Cook:
1. Set Zone One of the air fryer to 170ºC, select Bake, set the cook time to 3-5 minutes, or until crisp-tender. Drain well.
2. Select Zone Two and bake for 11 to 15 minutes, or until the strata is slightly puffy and set and the top starts to brown. Serve.

## Super Easy Bacon Cups & Southwestern Ham Egg Cups

**Prep time: 10 minutes | Cook time: 20 minutes | Serves 2-4**

### Bacon Cups:

- 3 slices bacon, cooked, sliced in half
- 2 slices ham
- 1 slice tomato
- 2 eggs
- 2 teaspoons grated Parmesan cheese
- Salt and ground black pepper, to taste

### Ham Egg Cups:

- 4 (30 g) slices wafer-thin ham
- 4 large eggs
- 2 tablespoons full-fat sour cream
- 60 g diced green pepper
- 2 tablespoons diced red pepper
- 2 tablespoons diced brown onion
- 120 g grated medium Cheddar cheese

**Prep for Bacon Cups:**

1. Line 2 greased muffin tins with 3 half-strips of bacon.
2. Put one slice of ham and half slice of tomato in each muffin tin on top of the bacon.
3. Crack one egg on top of the tomato in each muffin tin and sprinkle each with half a teaspoon of grated Parmesan cheese. Sprinkle with salt and ground black pepper, if desired.
4. Put the muffins in the drawer, and put into the Zone One of the air fryer.

**Prep for Ham Egg Cups:**

1. Place one slice of ham on the bottom of four baking cups.
2. In a large bowl, whisk eggs with sour cream. Stir in green pepper, red pepper, and onion.
3. Pour the egg mixture into ham-lined baking cups. Top with Cheddar. Place cups into the air fryer drawer.
4. Put the drawer in Zone Two.

**Cook:**

1. Set the Zone One of the air fryer to 190ºC, select bake, set the cook time to 20 minutes.
2. Set the Zone Two of the air fryer to 160ºC, select bake, set the cook time to 12 minutes.
3. Press SYNC, then press Start.
4. Cook until the surface of the food are slightly brown, remove from the air fryer and let cool. Serve warm.

## Golden Avocado Tempura & Italian Egg Cups

**Prep time: 10 minutes | Cook time: 10 minutes | Serves 2-4**

### Golden Avocado Tempura

- 60 g bread crumbs
- ½ teaspoons salt
- 1 Haas avocado, pitted, peeled and sliced
- Liquid from 1 can white beans

### Italian Egg Cups

- rapeseed oil
- 235 ml marinara sauce
- 4 eggs
- 4 tablespoons grated Cheddar cheese
- 4 teaspoons grated Parmesan cheese
- Salt and freshly ground black pepper, to taste
- Chopped fresh basil, for garnish

**Prep for Golden Avocado Tempura:**

1. Mix the bread crumbs and salt in a shallow bowl until well-incorporated.
2. Dip the avocado slices in the bean liquid, then into the bread crumbs.
3. Put the avocados in the Zone One of the air fryer and take care not to overlap any slices.

**Prep for Italian Egg Cups:**

1. Lightly spray 4 individual ramekins with rapeseed oil.
2. Pour 60 ml marinara sauce into each ramekin.
3. Crack one egg into each ramekin on top of the marinara sauce.
4. Sprinkle 1 tablespoon of Mozzarella and 1 tablespoon of Parmesan on top of each egg. Season with salt and pepper.
5. Cover each ramekin with aluminum foil. Place two of the ramekins in the Zone Two of the air fryer.
6. Repeat with the remaining two ramekins.

**Cook:**

1. Set the Zone One and Two of air fryer to 180ºC.
2. For Zone One, air fry for 10 minutes, giving the drawer a good shake at the halfway point.
3. Zone Two
    - Air fry for 5 minutes and remove the aluminum foil.
    - Air fry until the top is lightly browned and the egg white is cooked, another 2 to 4 minutes. If you prefer the yolk to be firmer, cook for 3 to 5 more minutes.
4. Garnish with basil and serve immediately.

# Cinnamon Rolls & Ham and Cheese Crescents

**Prep time: 15 minutes | Cook time: 20 minutes | Makes 8-12 rolls**

### Cinnamon Rolls

| | |
|---|---|
| 600 g grated Cheddar cheese | 96 ml icing sugar-style sweetener |
| 60 g soft cheese, softened | 1 tablespoon ground cinnamon |
| 120 g blanched finely ground almond flour | |
| ½ teaspoon vanilla extract | |

### Ham and Cheese Crescents

| | |
|---|---|
| Oil, for spraying | 8 cheese slices |
| 1 (230 g) can ready-to-bake croissants | 2 tablespoons unsalted butter, melted |
| 4 slices wafer-thin ham | |

**Prep for Cinnamon Rolls:**

1. In a large microwave-safe bowl, combine Cheddar cheese, soft cheese, and flour. Microwave the mixture on high 90 seconds until cheese is melted.
2. Add vanilla extract and sweetener, and mix 2 minutes until a dough forms.
3. Once the dough is cool enough to work with your hands, about 2 minutes, spread it out into a 12 × 4-inch rectangle on ungreased parchment paper. Evenly sprinkle dough with cinnamon.
4. Starting at the long side of the dough, roll lengthwise to form a log. Slice the log into twelve even pieces.
5. Divide rolls between two ungreased round nonstick baking dishes. Place one dish into the Zone One of the air fryer drawer.

**Prep for Ham and Cheese Crescents:**

1. Line the air fryer basket of Zone Two with parchment and spray lightly with oil.
2. Separate the dough into 8 pieces.
3. Tear the ham slices in half and place 1 piece on each piece of dough. Top each with 1 slice of cheese.
4. Roll up each piece of dough, starting on the wider side.
5. Place the rolls in the prepared basket. Brush with the melted butter.

**Cook:**

1. Adjust the Zone One to 190ºC, 10 minutes.
2. Select Zone Two, set 160ºC for 6 to 7 minutes, or until puffed and golden brown and the cheese is melted.
3. Press SYNC, then press Start
4. Cinnamon rolls will be done when golden around the edges and mostly firm. Repeat with second dish.
5. Allow rolls to cool in dishes 10 minutes before serving.

# Peppered Maple Bacon Knots & Smoky Sausage Patties

**Prep time: 35 minutes | Cook time: 9 minutes | Serves 6-8**

### Peppered Maple Bacon Knots

| | |
|---|---|
| 450 g maple smoked/cured bacon rashers | 48 g soft brown sugar |
| 60 ml maple syrup | Coarsely cracked black peppercorns, to taste |

### Smoky Sausage Patties

| | |
|---|---|
| 450 g pork mince | ½ teaspoon fennel seeds |
| 1 tablespoon soy sauce or tamari | ½ teaspoon dried thyme |
| 1 teaspoon smoked paprika | ½ teaspoon freshly ground black pepper |
| 1 teaspoon dried sage | ¼ teaspoon cayenne pepper |
| 1 teaspoon sea salt | |

**Prep for Peppered Maple Bacon Knots:**

1. On a clean work surface, tie each bacon strip in a loose knot.
2. Stir together the maple syrup and soft brown sugar in a bowl. Generously brush this mixture over the bacon knots.
3. Working in batches, arrange the bacon knots in the Zone One of air fryer. Sprinkle with the coarsely cracked black peppercorns.

**Prep for Smoky Sausage Patties:**

1. In a large bowl, combine the pork, soy sauce, smoked paprika, sage, salt, fennel seeds, thyme, black pepper, and cayenne pepper. Work the meat with your hands until the seasonings are fully incorporated.
2. Shape the mixture into 8 equal-size patties. Using your thumb, make a dent in the center of each patty. Place the patties on a plate and cover with plastic wrap. Refrigerate the patties for at least 30 minutes.
3. Working in batches if necessary, place the patties in a single layer in the Zone Two of air fryer, being careful not to overcrowd them.

**Cook:**

1. Preheat the air fryer to 200ºC.
2. Zone One
   - Air fry for 5 minutes. Flip the bacon knots and continue cooking for 2 to 3 minutes more, or until the bacon is crisp.
   - Remove from the basket to a paper towel-lined plate. Repeat with the remaining bacon knots.
   - Let the bacon knots cool for a few minutes and serve warm.
3. Zone One
   - Press Start for 5 minutes.
   - Flip and cook for about 4 minutes more.

## Onion Omelette & Spinach Omelet

**Prep time: 15 minutes | Cook time: 12 minutes | Serves 2-4**

### Onion Omelet:

| | |
|---|---|
| 3 eggs | 1 large onion, chopped |
| Salt and ground black pepper, to taste | 2 tablespoons grated Cheddar cheese |
| ½ teaspoons soy sauce | Cooking spray |

### Spinach Omelet

| | |
|---|---|
| 4 large eggs | 2 tablespoons salted butter, melted |
| 350 g chopped fresh spinach leaves | 120 g grated mild Cheddar cheese |
| 2 tablespoons peeled and chopped brown onion | ¼ teaspoon salt |

**Prep for Onion Omelet:**
1. In a bowl, whisk together the eggs, salt, pepper, and soy sauce.
2. Spritz a small pan with cooking spray. Spread the chopped onion across the bottom of the pan, then transfer the pan to the Zone One of the air fryer.

**Prep for Spinach Omelet:**
1. In an ungreased round nonstick baking dish, whisk eggs. Stir in spinach, onion, butter, Cheddar, and salt.
2. Place dish into the air fryer drawer in Zone Two.

**Cook:**
1. Set Zone One of the air fryer to 180ºC, select Bake, set the cook time to 12 minutes.
2. Press Match, set Zone Two of the air fryer to 160ºC.
3. Press Start, cook until the onion in Zone One is translucent. Add the egg mixture on top of the onions to coat well. Add the cheese on top, then continue baking for another 6 minutes.
4. Omelet will be done when browned on the top and firm in the middle. Slice in half and serve warm on two medium plates. Allow the onions to cool before serving.

## Sirloin Steaks with Eggs

**Prep time: 8 minutes | Cook time: 14 minutes per batch | Serves 4**

| | |
|---|---|
| Cooking oil spray | 1 teaspoon freshly ground black pepper, divided |
| 4 (110 g) sirloin steaks | |
| 1 teaspoon granulated garlic, divided | 4 eggs |
| | ½ teaspoon paprika |
| 1 teaspoon salt, divided | |

1. In a baking dish, combine the asparagus, carrot, red bell pepper, and 1 tablespoon of water into Zone One.
2. Add the bread cubes to the vegetables and gently toss.
3. In a medium bowl, whisk the egg whites, egg, milk, and thyme until frothy.
4. Pour the egg mixture into the pan of Zone Two.

**Cook:**
1. Insert the crisper plate into the drawer and the drawer into the unit. Set the unit by selecting AIR FRY, setting the temperature to 180ºC, and setting the time to 3 minutes. Select START/STOP to begin. 2. Once the unit is set, spray the crisper plate with cooking oil. Place 2 steaks into the drawer; do not oil or season them at this time. 3. Select AIR FRY, set the temperature to 180ºC, and set the time to 9 minutes. Select START/STOP to begin. 4. After 5 minutes, open the unit and flip the steaks. Sprinkle each with ¼ teaspoon of granulated garlic, ¼ teaspoon of salt, and ¼ teaspoon of pepper. Resume cooking until the steaks register at least 64ºC on a food thermometer. 5. When the cooking is complete, transfer the steaks to a plate and tent with aluminum foil to keep warm. Repeat steps 2, 3, and 4 with the remaining steaks. 6. Spray 4 ramekins with rapeseed oil. Crack 1 egg into each ramekin. Sprinkle the eggs with the paprika and remaining ½ teaspoon each of salt and pepper. Working in batches, place 2 ramekins into the drawer. 7. Select BAKE, set the temperature to 170ºC, and set the time to 5 minutes. Select START/STOP to begin. 8. When the cooking is complete and the eggs are cooked to 72ºC, remove the ramekins and repeat step 7 with the remaining 2 ramekins. 9. Serve the eggs with the steaks.

## Cauliflower Avocado Toast & Drop Biscuits

**Prep time: 15 minutes | Cook time: 9-10 minutes | Serves 2-5**

### Cauliflower Avocado Toast

| | |
|---|---|
| 1 (40 g) steamer bag cauliflower | ½ teaspoon garlic powder |
| 1 large egg | ¼ teaspoon ground black pepper |
| 120 g grated Cheddar cheese | 1 (40 g) steamer bag cauliflower |
| 1 ripe medium avocado | |

### Drop Biscuits

| | |
|---|---|
| 500 g plain flour | more for brushing on the biscuits (optional) |
| 1 tablespoon baking powder | |
| 1 tablespoon sugar (optional) | 180 ml buttermilk |
| 1 teaspoon salt | 1 to 2 tablespoons oil |
| 6 tablespoons butter, plus | |

### Prep for Cauliflower Avocado Toast
1. Cook cauliflower according to package instructions. Remove from bag and place into cheesecloth or clean towel to remove excess moisture.
2. Place cauliflower into a large bowl and mix in egg and Mozzarella. Cut a piece of parchment to fit your air fryer drawer. Separate the cauliflower mixture into two, and place it on the parchment in two mounds. Press out the cauliflower mounds into a ¼-inch-thick rectangle. Place the parchment into the Zone One of the air fryer.

### Prep for Drop Biscuits
3. In a large bowl, whisk the flour, baking powder, sugar (if using), and salt until blended.
4. Add the butter. Using a pastry cutter or 2 forks, work the dough until pea-size balls of the butter-flour mixture appear. Stir in the buttermilk until the mixture is sticky.
5. Line the Zone Two of the air fryer with parchment paper and spritz it with oil.

### Cook:
1. Adjust the temperature of Zone One to 200ºC and set the timer for 8 minutes. Set the Zone Two of the air fryer to 170ºC.
2. Drop the dough by the tablespoonful onto the prepared drawer, leaving 1 inch between each, to form 10 biscuits.
3. Bake for 5 minutes. Flip the biscuits and cook for 4 minutes more for a light brown top, or 5 minutes more for a darker biscuit. Brush the tops with melted butter, if desired.
4. Flip the cauliflower halfway through the cooking time.
5. When the timer beeps, remove the parchment and allow the cauliflower to cool 5 minutes.
6. Cut open the avocado and remove the pit. Scoop out the inside, place it in a medium bowl, and mash it with garlic powder and pepper. Spread onto the cauliflower. Serve immediately.

## Keto Quiche

**Prep time: 10 minutes | Cook time: 1 hour | Makes 1 (6-inch) quiche**

**Crust:**

| | |
|---|---|
| 150 g blanched almond flour | ¼ teaspoon fine sea salt |
| 300 g grated Parmesan or Gouda cheese | 1 large egg, beaten |

**Filling:**

| | |
|---|---|
| 120 g chicken or beef stock (or vegetable stock for vegetarian) | (about 110 g) |
| | 110 g soft cheese (120 ml) |
| 235 g grated Swiss cheese | 1 tablespoon unsalted butter, melted |
| 4 large eggs, beaten | ⅛ teaspoon cayenne pepper |
| 80 g minced leeks or sliced spring onions | Chopped spring onions, for garnish |
| ¾ teaspoon fine sea salt | |

### Prep for Crust
1. Grease a pie pan. Spray two large pieces of parchment paper with avocado oil and set them on the countertop.
2. In a medium-sized bowl, combine the flour, cheese, and salt and mix well. Add the egg and mix until the dough is well combined and stiff.
3. Place the dough in the center of one of the greased pieces of parchment. Top with the other piece of parchment. Using a rolling pin, roll out the dough into a circle about 1/16 inch thick.
4. Press the pie crust into the prepared pie pan and put the pie pan into Zone One of the air fryer.

### Prep for Filling
1. While the crust bakes, make the filling: In a large bowl, combine the stock, Swiss cheese, soft cheese, and butter.
2. Stir in the eggs, leeks, salt, and cayenne pepper.

### Cook:
1. Preheat the air fryer to 160ºC.
2. Place the prepared pie pan into the Zone One of air fryer and bake for 12 minutes, or until it starts to lightly brown.
3. When the crust is ready, pour the mixture into the crust of Zone Two.
4. Place the quiche in the Zone Two of the air fryer and bake for 15 minutes. Turn the heat down to 150ºC and bake for an additional 30 minutes, or until a knife inserted 1 inch from the edge comes out clean. You may have to cover the edges of the crust with foil to prevent burning.
5. Allow the quiche to cool for 10 minutes before garnishing it with chopped spring onions and cutting it into wedges.
6. Store leftovers in an airtight container in the refrigerator for up to 4 days or in the freezer for up to a month.
7. Reheat in a preheated 180ºC air fryer for a few minutes, until warmed through.

## Nutty Granola

**Prep time: 5 minutes | Cook time: 1 hour | Serves 4**

| | |
|---|---|
| 120 g pecans, roughly chopped | seeds |
| 120 g walnuts or almonds, roughly chopped | 2 tablespoons sunflower seeds |
| 60 g desiccated coconut | 2 tablespoons melted butter |
| 30 g almond flour | 60 ml granulated sweetener |
| 60 g ground flaxseed or chia | ½ teaspoon ground cinnamon |

Chapter 1  Breakfasts  | 9

½ teaspoon vanilla extract
¼ teaspoon ground nutmeg
¼ teaspoon salt
2 tablespoons water

1. Cut a piece of parchment paper to fit inside the air fryer basket.
2. In a large bowl, toss the nuts, coconut, almond flour, ground flaxseed or chia seeds, sunflower seeds, butter, sweetener, cinnamon, vanilla, nutmeg, salt, and water until thoroughly combined.
3. Spread the granola on the parchment paper and flatten to an even thickness.

Cook:
1. Preheat the air fryer to 120ºC.
2. Air fry for about an hour, or until golden throughout.
3. Remove from the air fryer and allow to fully cool.
4. Break the granola into bite-size pieces and store in a covered container for up to a week.

## Mississippi Spice Muffins & Cheddar-Ham-Corn Muffins

**Prep time: 25 minutes | Cook time: 13 minutes | Makes 8-12 muffins**

### Mississippi Spice Muffins

| | |
|---|---|
| 1 kg plain | temperature |
| 1 tablespoon ground cinnamon | 350 g sugar |
| 2 teaspoons baking soda | 2 large eggs, lightly beaten |
| 2 teaspoons allspice | 475 ml unsweetened applesauce |
| 1 teaspoon ground cloves | 60 g chopped pecans |
| 1 teaspoon salt | 1 to 2 tablespoons oil |
| 235 g (2 sticks) butter, room | |

### Cheddar-Ham-Corn Muffins

| | |
|---|---|
| 90 g cornmeal/polenta | 120 g grated mature Cheddar cheese |
| 30 g flour | 120 g diced gammon |
| 1½ teaspoons baking powder | 8 foil muffin cups, liners removed and sprayed with cooking spray |
| ¼ teaspoon salt | |
| 1 egg, beaten | |
| 2 tablespoons rapeseed oil | |
| 120 ml milk | |

Prep for Mississippi Spice Muffins
1. In a large bowl, whisk the flour, cinnamon, baking soda, allspice, cloves, and salt until blended.
2. In another large bowl, combine the butter and sugar. Using an electric mixer, beat the mixture for 2 to 3 minutes until light and fluffy. Add the beaten eggs and stir until blended.
3. Add the flour mixture and applesauce, alternating between the two and blending after each addition. Stir in the pecans.
4. Spritz 12 silicone muffin cups with oil.
5. Pour the batter into the prepared muffin cups, filling each halfway. Place the muffins in the Zone One of the air fryer.

Prep for Cheddar-Ham-Corn Muffins
1. In a medium bowl, stir together the cornmeal, flour, baking powder, and salt.
2. Add egg, oil, and milk to dry ingredients and mix well.
3. Stir in grated cheese and diced gammon.
4. Divide batter among the muffin cups.
5. Place 4 filled muffin cups in Zone Two of the air fryer drawer and bake for 5 minutes.

Cook:
1. Select Zone One, set the air fryer to 160ºC, 6 minutes.
2. Select Zone Two, set the air fryer to 200ºC, 5 minutes.
3. Press Sync, then press Start.
4. Shake the Zone One and air fry for 7 minutes more. The muffins are done when a toothpick inserted into the middle comes out clean.
5. Reduce temperature of Zone Two to 170ºC and bake for 1 to 2 minutes or until toothpick inserted in center of muffin comes out clean. Repeat steps 6 and 7 to cook remaining muffins.

## BLT Breakfast Wrap & Meritage Eggs

**Prep time: 10 minutes | Cook time: 10 minutes | Serves 4-6**

### BLT Wrap:

| | |
|---|---|
| 230 g reduced-salt bacon | 4 vine tomatoes, sliced |
| 8 tablespoons mayonnaise | Salt and freshly ground black pepper, to taste |
| 8 large romaine lettuce leaves | |

### Meritage Eggs:

| | |
|---|---|
| 2 teaspoons unsalted butter (or coconut oil for dairy-free), for greasing the ramekins | 2 tablespoons double cream (or unsweetened, unflavoured almond milk for dairy-free) |
| 4 large eggs | 3 tablespoons finely grated Parmesan cheese (or chive soft cheese style spread, softened, for dairy-free) |
| 2 teaspoons chopped fresh thyme | |
| ½ teaspoon fine sea salt | |
| ¼ teaspoon ground black pepper | Fresh thyme leaves, for garnish (optional) |

Prep for BLT Wrap:
Arrange the bacon in a single layer in the air fryer drawer of Zone One. (It's OK if the bacon sits a bit on the sides.)

### Prep for Meritage Eggs:
1. Grease two (110 g) ramekins with the butter.
2. Crack 2 eggs into each ramekin and divide the thyme, salt, and pepper between the ramekins. Pour 1 tablespoon of the heavy cream into each ramekin. Sprinkle each ramekin with 1½ tablespoons of the Parmesan cheese.
3. Place the ramekins in the drawer of Zone Two.

### Cook:
1. Set the Zone One of the air fryer to 180°C, select Air Fry, set the cook time to 10 minutes.
2. Set the Zone Two of the air fryer to 200°C, select Bake, set the cook time to 8 minutes.
3. Press Sync, then press START.
4. Check for crispiness in Zone One and air fry for 2 to 3 minutes longer if needed. Spread 1 tablespoon of mayonnaise on each of the lettuce leaves and top with the tomatoes and cooked bacon. Season to taste with salt and freshly ground black pepper. Roll the lettuce leaves as you would a burrito, securing with a toothpick if desired.
5. Cook in Zone Two for soft-cooked yolks (longer if you desire a harder yolk). Garnish with a sprinkle of ground black pepper and thyme leaves, if desired. Best served fresh.

## Breakfast Sausage and Cauliflower & Vanilla Granola

**Prep time: 10 minutes | Cook time: 45 minutes | Serves 4**

### Breakfast Sausage and Cauliflower
- 450 g sausage meat, cooked and crumbled
- 475 ml double/whipping cream
- 1 head cauliflower, chopped
- 235 g grated Cheddar cheese, plus more for topping
- 8 eggs, beaten
- Salt and ground black pepper, to taste

### Vanilla Granola
- 235 g porridge oats
- 3 tablespoons maple syrup
- 1 tablespoon sunflower oil
- 1 tablespoon coconut sugar
- ¼ teaspoon vanilla
- ¼ teaspoon cinnamon
- ¼ teaspoon sea salt

### Prep for Breakfast Sausage and Cauliflower:
1. In a large bowl, mix the sausage, cream, chopped cauliflower, cheese and eggs. Sprinkle with salt and ground black pepper.
2. Pour the mixture into a greased casserole dish and put the dish into Zone One of air fryer.

### Prep for Vanilla Granola:
1. Mix together the oats, maple syrup, sunflower oil, coconut sugar, vanilla, cinnamon, and sea salt in a medium bowl and stir to combine.
2. Transfer the mixture to a baking pan and put it into Zone Two of the air fryer.

### Cook:
1. Preheat the air fryer to 200°C.
2. Select Zone One, set 45 minutes or until firm.
3. Select Zone Two, set 40 minutes, or until the granola is mostly dry and lightly browned.
4. Press Sync, then press Start.
5. Stir the granola four times during cooking.
6. Top with more Cheddar cheese and serve. Let the granola stand for 5 to 10 minutes before serving.

# Chapter 2　Family Favorites

## Filo Vegetable Triangles & Old Bay Tilapia

**Prep time: 30 minutes | Cook time: 6 to 11 minutes | Serves 4-6**

### Filo Vegetable Triangles

| | |
|---|---|
| 3 tablespoons finely chopped onion | 2 tablespoons fat-free soft white cheese, at room temperature |
| 2 garlic cloves, minced | |
| 2 tablespoons grated carrot | 6 sheets frozen filo pastry, thawed |
| 1 teaspoon olive oil | |
| 3 tablespoons frozen baby peas, thawed | Olive oil spray, for coating the dough |

### Old Bay Tilapia

| | |
|---|---|
| Oil, for spraying | ½ teaspoon salt |
| 235 ml panko breadcrumbs | ¼ teaspoon freshly ground black pepper |
| 2 tablespoons Old Bay or all-purpose seasoning | 1 large egg |
| 2 teaspoons granulated garlic | 4 tilapia fillets |
| 1 teaspoon onion powder | |

Prep for Filo Vegetable Triangles
1. In Zone One, combine the onion, garlic, carrot, and olive oil.
2. Transfer vegetables to a bowl.
3. Stir in the peas and soft white cheese to the vegetable mixture. Let cool while you prepare the dough.
4. Lay one sheet of filo on a work surface and lightly spray with olive oil spray.
5. Top with another sheet of filo. Repeat with the remaining 4 filo sheets; you'll have 3 stacks with 2 layers each.
6. Cut each stack lengthwise into 4 strips (12 strips total). Place a scant 2 teaspoons of the filling near the bottom of each strip.
7. Bring one corner up over the filling to make a triangle; continue folding the triangles over, as you would fold a flag.
8. Seal the edge with a bit of water. Repeat with the remaining strips and filling.

Prep for Old Bay Tilapia
1. Line the Zone Two of the air fry with parchment and spray lightly with oil. In a shallow bowl, mix together the breadcrumbs, seasoning, garlic, onion powder, salt, and black pepper.
2. In a small bowl, whisk the egg. Coat the tilapia in the egg, then dredge in the bread crumb mixture until completely coated.
3. Place the tilapia in the prepared drawer. You may need to work in batches, depending on the size of your air fryer. Spray lightly with oil.

Cook:
1. Set Zone One at 200°C for 2 to 4 minutes, or until the vegetables are crisp-tender.
2. Set the Zone Two of the air fryer to 200°C. Cook for 4 to 6 minutes, depending on the thickness of the fillets, until the internal temperature reaches 60°C.
3. Air fry the triangles in the Zone Two, in 2 batches, for 4 to 7 minutes, or until golden brown.
4. Serve immediately.

## Mixed Berry Crumble & Scallops with Green Vegetables

**Prep time: 25 minutes | Cook time: 11 to 16 minutes | Serves 4**

### Mixed Berry Crumble

| | |
|---|---|
| 120 g chopped fresh strawberries | 1 tablespoon honey |
| | 80 g wholemeal plain flour |
| 120 g fresh blueberries | 3 tablespoons light muscovado sugar |
| 80 g frozen raspberries | |
| 1 tablespoon freshly squeezed lemon juice | 2 tablespoons unsalted butter, melted |

### Scallops with Green Vegetables

| | |
|---|---|
| 235 g green beans | 2 teaspoons olive oil |
| 235 g garden peas | ½ teaspoon dried basil |
| 235 g frozen chopped broccoli | ½ teaspoon dried oregano |
| | 340 g sea scallops |

Prep for Mixed Berry Crumble
1. In Zone One of the air fry, combine the strawberries, blueberries, and raspberries.
2. Drizzle with the lemon juice and honey.
3. In a small bowl, mix the pastry flour and brown sugar.
4. Stir in the butter and mix until crumbly.
5. Sprinkle this mixture over the fruit.

Prep for Scallops with Green Vegetables
1. In a large bowl, toss the green beans, peas, and broccoli with the olive oil.
2. Place in the Zone Two of the air fryer.

Cook:
1. Bake Zone One at 190°C for 11 to 16 minutes, or until the fruit is tender and bubbly and the topping is golden brown.
2. Bake Zone Two at 200°C for 4 to 6 minutes, or until the vegetables are crisp-tender.
3. Remove the vegetables from the air fryer drawer and sprinkle with the herbs. Set aside.
4. In the Zone Two, put the scallops and air fry for 4 to 5

minutes, or until the scallops are firm and reach an internal temperature of just 64°C on a meat thermometer.
5. Toss scallops with the vegetables and serve immediately with warm Berry Crumble.

## Beef Jerky

**Prep time: 30 minutes | Cook time: 2 hours | Serves 8**

### Oil, for spraying

| | |
|---|---|
| 450 g silverside, cut into thin, short slices | muscovado sugar |
| 60 ml soy sauce | 1 tablespoon minced garlic |
| 3 tablespoons packed light | 1 teaspoon ground ginger |
| | 1 tablespoon water |

1. Line the air fryer drawer with parchment and spray lightly with oil.
2. Place the steak, soy sauce, brown sugar, garlic, ginger, and water in a zip-top plastic bag, seal, and shake well until evenly coated.
3. Refrigerate for 30 minutes. Divide the steak into two parts and place them in the prepared Zone One and Zone Two respectively.

Cook:
1. Air fry at 80°C for at least 2 hours.
2. Add more time if you like your jerky a bit tougher.

## Beignets & Churro Bites

**Prep time: 35 minutes | Cook time: 6 minutes | Makes 9 beignets and 36 Bites**

### Beignets:

| | |
|---|---|
| Oil, for greasing and spraying | 235 ml milk |
| 350 g plain flour, plus more for dusting | 2 tablespoons packed light muscovado sugar |
| 1½ teaspoons salt | 1 tablespoon unsalted butter |
| 1 (2¼-teaspoon) instant yeast | 1 large egg |
| | 180 g icing sugar |

### Churro:

| | |
|---|---|
| Oil, for spraying | 1 tablespoon ground cinnamon |
| 1 (500 g) package frozen puffed pastry, thawed | 90 g icing sugar |
| 180 g caster sugar | 1 tablespoon milk |

Prep for Beignets:
1. Oil a large bowl. In a small bowl, mix together the flour, salt, and yeast. Set aside. Pour the milk into a glass measuring cup and microwave in 1-minute intervals until it boils. 2.In a large bowl, mix together the brown sugar and butter. 3.Pour in the hot milk and whisk until the sugar has dissolved. Let cool to room temperature. 4.Whisk the egg into the cooled milk mixture and fold in the flour mixture until a dough form. 5.On a lightly floured work surface, knead the dough for 3 to 5 minutes. 6.Place the dough in the oiled bowl and cover with a clean kitchen towel. Let rise in a warm place for about 1 hour, or until doubled in size. 7.Roll the dough out on a lightly floured work surface until it's about ¼ inch thick. 8.Cut the dough into 3-inch squares and place them on a lightly floured baking sheet. 9.Cover loosely with a kitchen towel and let rise again until doubled in size, about 30 minutes. 10.Line the air fryer drawer with parchment and spray lightly with oil. 11.Place the dough squares in the Zone One drawer and spray lightly with oil.

Prep for Churro:
1. Line the air fryer drawer with parchment and spray lightly with oil. 2.Unfold the puff pastry onto a clean work surface. Using a sharp knife, cut the dough into 36 bite-size pieces. 3.Place the dough pieces in one layer in the Zone Two drawer, taking care not to let the pieces touch or overlap.

Cook:
1. Set Zone One to 200°C, select Air fry, set the cook time to 6 minutes.
2. Press MATCH, then Press START.
3. Cook for 3 minutes, flip the food in both units, spray with oil, and cook for another 3 minutes, until the beignets are crispy and the churros are golden.
4. Dust the beignets with the icing sugar before serving.
5. In a small bowl, mix together the caster sugar and cinnamon. In another small bowl, whisk together the icing sugar and milk. Dredge the churro bites in the cinnamon-sugar mixture until evenly coated. Serve with the icing on the side for dipping.

## Pork Burgers with Red Cabbage Salad & Berry Cheesecake

**Prep time: 25 minutes | Cook time: 10 minutes | Serves 4**

### Pork Burgers with Red Cabbage Salad

| | |
|---|---|
| 120 ml Greek yoghurt | pork |
| 2 tablespoons low-salt mustard, divided | ½ teaspoon paprika |
| 1 tablespoon lemon juice | 235 g mixed salad leaves |
| 60 g sliced red cabbage | 2 small tomatoes, sliced |
| 60 g grated carrots | 8 small low-salt wholemeal sandwich buns, cut in half |
| 450 g lean finely chopped | |

14 | Chapter 2  Family Favorites

**Berry Cheesecake**

| | |
|---|---|
| Oil, for spraying | 1 large egg |
| 227 g soft white cheese | ½ teaspoon vanilla extract |
| 6 tablespoons sugar | ¼ teaspoon lemon juice |
| 1 tablespoon sour cream | 120 g fresh mixed berries |

### Prep for Pork Burgers with Red Cabbage Salad

1. In a small bowl, combine the yoghurt, 1 tablespoon mustard, lemon juice, cabbage, and carrots; mix and refrigerate.
2. In a medium bowl, combine the pork, remaining 1 tablespoon mustard, and paprika. form into 8 small patties. Put the sliders into the Zone One of the air fryer.

### Prep for Berry Cheesecake

1. Line the air fryer drawer with parchment and spray lightly with oil.
2. In a blender, combine the soft white cheese, sugar, sour cream, egg, vanilla, and lemon juice and blend until smooth.
3. Pour the mixture into a 4-inch springform pan.

### Cook:

1. Set the Zone Two to 180°C. Place the pan in the prepared drawer. Cook for 8 to 10 minutes, or until only the very centre jiggles slightly when the pan is moved.
2. Set the Zone One to 200°C for 7 to 9 minutes, or until the sliders register 74°C as tested with a meat thermometer.
3. Assemble the burgers by placing some of the lettuce greens on a bun bottom.
4. Top with a tomato slice, the burgers, and the cabbage mixture.
5. Add the bun top and serve immediately.
6. Refrigerate the cheesecake in the pan for at least 2 hours.
7. Release the sides from the springform pan, top the cheesecake with the mixed berries, and serve.

# Chapter 3    Fast and Easy Every-day Favourites

## Indian-Style Sweet Potato Fries

**Prep time: 10 minutes | Cook time: 8 minutes | Makes 20 fries |**

**Serves 1**

| | |
|---|---|
| Seasoning Mixture: | pepper |
| ¾ teaspoon ground coriander | Fries: |
| ½ teaspoon garam masala | 2 large sweet potatoes, peeled |
| ½ teaspoon garlic powder | 2 teaspoons olive oil |
| ½ teaspoon ground cumin | |
| ¼ teaspoon ground cayenne | |

Cook:
1. Set the air fryer to 200°C.
2. In a small bowl, combine the coriander, garam masala, garlic powder, cumin, and cayenne pepper.
3. Slice the sweet potatoes into ¼-inch-thick fries. In a large bowl, toss the sliced sweet potatoes with the olive oil and the seasoning mixture.
4. Transfer the seasoned sweet potatoes to the air fryer drawer and fry for 8 minutes, until crispy.
5. Serve warm.

## Cheesy Potato Patties

**Prep time: 5 minutes | Cook time: 10 minutes | Serves 8**

| | |
|---|---|
| 900 g white potatoes | 1 tablespoon fine sea salt |
| 120 g finely chopped spring onions | ½ teaspoon hot paprika |
| ½ teaspoon freshly ground black pepper, or more to taste | 475 g shredded Colby or Monterey Jack cheese |
| | 60 ml rapeseed oil |
| | 235 g crushed crackers |

Cook:
1. Set the air fryer to 180°C. Boil the potatoes until soft.
2. Dry them off and peel them before mashing thoroughly, leaving no lumps.
3. Combine the mashed potatoes with spring onions, pepper, salt, paprika, and cheese.
4. Mould the mixture into balls with your hands and press with your palm to flatten them into patties.
5. In a shallow dish, combine the rapeseed oil and crushed crackers.
6. Coat the patties in the crumb mixture.
7. Bake the patties for about 10 minutes, in multiple batches if necessary.
8. Serve hot.

## Beetroot Salad with Lemon Vinaigrette

**Prep time: 10 minutes | Cook time: 12 to 15 minutes | Serves 4**

| | |
|---|---|
| 6 medium red and golden beetroots, peeled and sliced | Cooking spray |
| 1 teaspoon olive oil | Vinaigrette: |
| ¼ teaspoon rock salt | 2 teaspoons olive oil |
| 120 g crumbled feta cheese | 2 tablespoons chopped fresh chives |
| 2 kg mixed greens | Juice of 1 lemon |

Cook:
1. Set the air fryer to 180°C.
2. In a large bowl, toss the beetroots, olive oil, and rock salt.
3. Spray the air fryer drawer with cooking spray, then place the beetroots in the drawer and air fry for 12 to 15 minutes or until tender.
4. While the beetroots cook, make the vinaigrette in a large bowl by whisking together the olive oil, lemon juice, and chives.
5. Remove the beetroots from the air fryer, toss in the vinaigrette, and allow to cool for 5 minutes.
6. Add the feta and serve on top of the mixed greens.

## Scalloped Veggie Mix

**Prep time: 10 minutes | Cook time: 15 minutes | Serves 4**

| | |
|---|---|
| 1 Yukon Gold or other small white potato, thinly sliced | 60 g minced onion |
| 1 small sweet potato, peeled and thinly sliced | 3 garlic cloves, minced |
| | 180 ml 2 percent milk |
| 1 medium carrot, thinly sliced | 2 tablespoons cornflour |
| | ½ teaspoon dried thyme |

Cook:
1. Set the air fryer to 190°C.
2. In a baking tray, layer the potato, sweet potato, carrot, onion, and garlic.
3. In a small bowl, whisk the milk, cornflour, and thyme until blended.
4. Pour the milk mixture evenly over the vegetables in the pan. Bake for 15 minutes.
5. Check the casserole—it should be golden brown on top, and the vegetables should be tender.
6. Serve immediately.

## Herb-Roasted Veggies

**Prep time: 10 minutes | Cook time: 14 to 18 minutes | Serves 4**

| | |
|---|---|
| 1 red pepper, sliced | 80 g diced red onion |
| 1 (230 g) package sliced mushrooms | 3 garlic cloves, sliced |
| | 1 teaspoon olive oil |
| 235 g green beans, cut into 2-inch pieces | ½ teaspoon dried basil |
| | ½ teaspoon dried tarragon |

Cook:
1. Set the air fryer to 180ºC.
2. In a medium bowl, mix the red pepper, mushrooms, green beans, red onion, and garlic.
3. Drizzle with the olive oil. Toss to coat.
4. Add the herbs and toss again. Place the vegetables in the air fryer drawer.
5. Roast for 14 to 18 minutes, or until tender.
6. Serve immediately.

## Purple Potato Chips with Rosemary

**Prep time: 10 minutes | Cook time: 9 to 14 minutes | Serves 6**

| | |
|---|---|
| 235 ml Greek yoghurt | miniature potatoes |
| 2 chipotle chillies, minced | 1 teaspoon olive oil |
| 2 tablespoons adobo or chipotle sauce | 2 teaspoons minced fresh rosemary leaves |
| 1 teaspoon paprika | ⅛ teaspoon cayenne pepper |
| 1 tablespoon lemon juice | ¼ teaspoon coarse sea salt |
| 10 purple fingerling or | |

Cook:
1. Set the air fryer to 200ºC.
2. In a medium bowl, combine the yoghurt, minced chillies, adobo sauce, paprika, and lemon juice. Mix well and refrigerate.
3. Wash the potatoes and dry them with paper towels.
4. Slice the potatoes lengthwise, as thinly as possible. You can use a mandoline, a vegetable peeler, or a very sharp knife.
5. Combine the potato slices in a medium bowl and drizzle with the olive oil; toss to coat.
6. Air fry the chips, in batches, in the air fryer drawer, for 9 to 14 minutes.
7. Use tongs to gently rearrange the chips halfway during cooking time.
8. Sprinkle the chips with the rosemary, cayenne pepper, and sea salt.
9. Serve with the chipotle sauce for dipping.

## Beery and Crunchy Onion Rings

**Prep time: 10 minutes | Cook time: 16 minutes | Serves 2 to 4**

| | |
|---|---|
| 80 g plain flour | 180 ml beer |
| 1 teaspoon paprika | 175 g breadcrumbs |
| ½ teaspoon bicarbonate of soda | 1 tablespoons olive oil |
| 1 teaspoon salt | 1 large Vidalia or sweet onion, peeled and sliced into ½-inch rings |
| ½ teaspoon freshly ground black pepper | Cooking spray |
| 1 egg, beaten | |

Cook:
1. Set the air fryer to 180ºC.
2. Spritz the air fryer drawer with cooking spray. Combine the flour, paprika, bicarbonate of soda, salt, and ground black pepper in a bowl.
3. Stir to mix well. Combine the egg and beer in a separate bowl.
4. Stir to mix well. Make a well in the centre of the flour mixture, then pour the egg mixture in the well.
5. Stir to mix everything well. Pour the breadcrumbs and olive oil in a shallow plate. Stir to mix well.
6. Dredge the onion rings gently into the flour and egg mixture, then shake the excess off and put into the plate of breadcrumbs.
7. Flip to coat both sides well. Arrange the onion rings in the set air fryer.
8. Air fry in batches for 16 minutes or until golden brown and crunchy.
9. Flip the rings and put the bottom rings to the top halfway through.
10. Serve immediately.

## Rosemary and Orange Roasted Chickpeas

**Prep time: 5 minutes | Cook time: 10 to 12 minutes | Makes 1 L**

| | |
|---|---|
| 1 kg cooked chickpeas | 1 teaspoon paprika |
| 2 tablespoons vegetable oil | Zest of 1 orange |
| 1 teaspoon rock salt | 1 tablespoon chopped fresh rosemary |
| 1 teaspoon cumin | |

Cook:
1. Set the air fryer to 200ºC.
2. Make sure the chickpeas are completely dry prior to roasting. In a medium bowl, toss the chickpeas with oil, salt, cumin, and paprika.

3. Working in batches, spread the chickpeas in a single layer in the air fryer drawer.
4. Air fry for 10 to 12 minutes until crisp, shaking once halfway through.
5. Return the warm chickpeas to the bowl and toss with the orange zest and rosemary.
6. Allow to cool completely. Serve.

## Buttery Sweet Potatoes

**Prep time: 5 minutes | Cook time: 10 minutes | Serves 4**

| | |
|---|---|
| 2 tablespoons melted butter | 2 sweet potatoes, peeled and cut into ½-inch cubes |
| 1 tablespoon light brown sugar | Cooking spray |

Cook:
1. Set the air fryer to 200ºC.
2. Line the air fryer drawer with parchment paper. In a medium bowl, stir together the melted butter and brown sugar until blended.
3. Toss the sweet potatoes in the butter mixture until coated. Place the sweet potatoes on the parchment and spritz with oil.
4. Air fry for 5 minutes. Shake the drawer, spritz the sweet potatoes with oil, and air fry for 5 minutes more until they're soft enough to cut with a fork.
5. Serve immediately.

## Air Fried Tortilla Chips & Spinach and Carrot Balls

**Prep time: 15 minutes | Cook time: 10 minutes | Serves 4-6**

**Tortilla Chips:**

| | |
|---|---|
| 4 six-inch corn tortillas, cut in half and slice into thirds | ¼ teaspoon rock salt |
| 1 tablespoon rapeseed oil | Cooking spray |

**Spinach and Carrot Balls:**

| | |
|---|---|
| 2 slices toasted bread | 1 teaspoon minced garlic |
| 1 carrot, peeled and grated | 1 teaspoon salt |
| 1 package fresh spinach, blanched and chopped | ½ teaspoon black pepper |
| ½ onion, chopped | 1 tablespoon Engevita yeast flakes |
| 1 egg, beaten | 1 tablespoon flour |
| ½ teaspoon garlic powder | |

Prep for Tortilla Chips:
1. Spritz the air fryer drawer in Zone One with cooking spray. 2. On a clean work surface, brush the tortilla chips with rapeseed oil, then transfer the chips in the set air fryer.

Prep for Spinach and Carrot Balls:
1. In a food processor, pulse the toasted bread to form breadcrumbs. 3.Transfer into a shallow dish or bowl. In a bowl, mix together all the other ingredients. 4.Use your hands to shape the mixture into small-sized balls. 5.Roll the balls in the breadcrumbs, ensuring to cover them well. 6.Put in the air fryer drawer of Zone Two.

Cook:
1. Set the Zone One of air fryer to 180ºC, select Air fry, set the cook time to 10 minutes. 2. Press MATCH, set the Zone Two of air fryer to 200ºC.
3. Press Sync, then press Start.
4. Cook until the chips are crunchy and lightly browned. Shake the drawer and sprinkle with salt halfway through the cooking time. Transfer the chips onto a plate lined with paper towels. Serve immediately.

## Simple and Easy Croutons & Bacon Pinwheels

**Prep time: 15 minutes | Cook time: 10 minutes | Serves 4-6**

**Croutons:**

| | |
|---|---|
| 2 sliced bread | Hot soup, for serving |
| 1 tablespoon olive oil | |

**Bacon:**

| | |
|---|---|
| 1 sheet puff pastry | 8 slices bacon |
| 2 tablespoons maple syrup | Ground black pepper, to taste |
| 48 g brown sugar | Cooking spray |

Prep for Croutons:
1. Cut the slices of bread into medium-size chunks. 3.Brush the air fryer drawer with the oil. 4.Place the chunks inside Zone One.

Prep for Bacon:
1. Spritz the air fryer drawer in Zone Two with cooking spray. 2.Roll the puff pastry into a 10-inch square with a rolling pin on a clean work surface, then cut the pastry into 8 strips. 3.Brush the strips with maple syrup and sprinkle with sugar, leaving a 1-inch far end uncovered. 4.Arrange each slice of bacon on each strip, leaving a ⅛-inch length of bacon hang over the end close to you. Sprinkle with black pepper. 5.From the end close to you, roll the strips into pinwheels, then dab the uncovered end with water and seal the rolls. 6.Arrange the pinwheels in

the Zone Two of air fryer and spritz with cooking spray.

Cook:
1. Set Zone One of the air fryer to 200°C, select Air Fry, Set the cook time to 8 minutes.
2. Press MATCH, set Zone Two to 180°C, set the cook time to 10 minutes.
3. Press Sync, then press START. Flip the pinwheels halfway through. Serve immediately.

## Cheesy Chilli Toast

**Prep time: 5 minutes | Cook time: 5 minutes | Serves 1**

- 2 tablespoons grated Parmesan cheese
- 2 tablespoons grated Mozzarella cheese
- 2 teaspoons salted butter, at room temperature
- 10 to 15 thin slices serrano chilli or jalapeño
- 2 slices sourdough bread
- ½ teaspoon black pepper

Cook:
1. Set the air fryer to 160°C.
2. In a small bowl, stir together the Parmesan, Mozzarella, butter, and chillies.
3. Spread half the mixture onto one side of each slice of bread.
4. Sprinkle with the pepper.
5. Place the slices, cheese-side up, in the air fryer drawer.
6. Bake for 5 minutes, or until the cheese has melted and started to brown slightly.
7. Serve immediately.

# Chapter 4  Poultry

## Spice-Rubbed Turkey Breast

**Prep time: 5 minutes | Cook time: 45 to 55 minutes | Serves 10**

| | |
|---|---|
| 1 tablespoon sea salt | black pepper |
| 1 teaspoon paprika | 1.8 kg bone-in, skin-on turkey breast |
| 1 teaspoon onion powder | |
| 1 teaspoon garlic powder | 2 tablespoons unsalted butter, melted |
| ½ teaspoon freshly ground | |

Cook:

1. In a small bowl, combine the salt, paprika, onion powder, garlic powder, and pepper.
2. Sprinkle the seasonings all over the turkey. Brush the turkey with some of the melted butter.
3. Set the air fryer to 180°C. . Place the turkey in the air fryer drawer, skin-side down, and roast for 25 minutes.
4. Flip the turkey and brush it with the remaining butter. Continue cooking for another 20 to 30 minutes, until an instant-read thermometer reads 70°C.
5. Remove the turkey breast from the air fryer. Tent a piece of aluminum foil over the turkey, and allow it to rest for about 5 minutes before serving.

## Crunchy Chicken with Roasted Carrots

**Prep time: 10 minutes | Cook time: 22 minutes | Serves 4**

| | |
|---|---|
| 4 bone-in, skin-on chicken thighs | 2 teaspoons poultry spice |
| | 1 teaspoon sea salt, divided |
| 2 carrots, cut into 2-inch pieces | 2 teaspoons chopped fresh rosemary leaves |
| 2 tablespoons extra-virgin olive oil | Cooking oil spray |
| | 500 g cooked white rice |

Cook:

1. Brush the chicken thighs and carrots with olive oil. Sprinkle both with the poultry spice, salt, and rosemary.
2. Insert the crisper plate into the drawer and the drawer into the unit. Set the unit by selecting AIR FRY, setting the temperature to 200°C, and setting the time to 3 minutes. Select START/STOP to begin.
3. Once the unit is set, spray the crisper plate with cooking oil. Place the carrots into the drawer. Add the wire rack and arrange the chicken thighs on the rack.
4. Select AIR FRY, set the temperature to 200°C, and set the time to 20 minutes. Select START/STOP to begin.
5. When the cooking is complete, check the chicken temperature. If a food thermometer inserted into the chicken registers 76°C, remove the chicken from the air fryer, place it on a clean plate, and cover with aluminum foil to keep warm. Otherwise, resume cooking for 1 to 2 minutes longer.
6. The carrots can cook for 18 to 22 minutes and will be tender and caramelized; cooking time isn't as crucial for root vegetables.
7. Serve the chicken and carrots with the hot cooked rice.

## Easy Turkey Tenderloin

**Prep time: 20 minutes | Cook time: 30 minutes | Serves 4**

| | |
|---|---|
| Olive oil | black pepper |
| ½ teaspoon paprika | Pinch cayenne pepper |
| ½ teaspoon garlic powder | 680 g turkey breast tenderloin |
| ½ teaspoon salt | |
| ½ teaspoon freshly ground | |

Cook:

1. Spray the air fryer drawer lightly with olive oil.
2. In a small bowl, combine the paprika, garlic powder, salt, black pepper, and cayenne pepper. Rub the mixture all over the turkey.
3. Place the turkey in the air fryer drawer and lightly spray with olive oil.
4. Air fry at 190°C for 15 minutes. Flip the turkey over and lightly spray with olive oil. Air fry until the internal temperature reaches at least 80°C for an additional 10 to 15 minutes.
5. Let the turkey rest for 10 minutes before slicing and serving.

## Peanut Butter Chicken Satay

**Prep time: 12 minutes | Cook time: 12 to 18 minutes | Serves 4**

| | |
|---|---|
| 120 g crunchy peanut butter | 2 garlic cloves, minced |
| 80 ml chicken broth | 2 tablespoons extra-virgin olive oil |
| 3 tablespoons low-sodium soy sauce | |
| | 1 teaspoon curry powder |
| 2 tablespoons freshly squeezed lemon juice | 450 g chicken tenders |
| | Cooking oil spray |

Cook:

1. In a medium bowl, whisk the peanut butter, broth, soy sauce, lemon juice, garlic, olive oil, and curry powder until smooth.
2. Place 2 tablespoons of this mixture into a small bowl. Transfer the remaining sauce to a serving bowl and set aside.
3. Add the chicken tenders to the bowl with the 2 tablespoons of sauce and stir to coat. Let stand for a few minutes to marinate.

4. Insert the crisper plate into the drawer and the drawer into the unit. Set the unit by selecting AIR FRY, setting the temperature to 200°C, and setting the time to 3 minutes. Select START/STOP to begin.
5. Run a 6-inch bamboo skewer lengthwise through each chicken tender.
6. Once the unit is set, spray the crisper plate with cooking oil. Working in batches, place half the chicken skewers into the drawer in a single layer without overlapping.
7. Select AIR FRY, set the temperature to 200°C, and set the time to 9 minutes. Select START/STOP to begin.
8. After 6 minutes, check the chicken. If a food thermometer inserted into the chicken registers 76°C, it is done. If not, resume cooking.
9. Repeat steps 6, 7, and 8 with the remaining chicken.
10. When the cooking is complete, serve the chicken with the reserved sauce.

## Chicken Hand Pies

**Prep time: 30 minutes | Cook time: 10 minutes per batch | Makes 8 pies**

| | |
|---|---|
| 180 ml chicken broth | 1 tablespoon milk |
| 130 g frozen mixed peas and carrots | Salt and pepper, to taste |
| 140 g cooked chicken, chopped | 1 (8-count) can organic flaky biscuits |
| 1 tablespoon cornflour | Oil for misting or cooking spray |

Cook:
1. In a medium saucepan, bring chicken broth to a boil. Stir in the frozen peas and carrots and cook for 5 minutes over medium heat. Stir in chicken.
2. Mix the cornflour into the milk until it dissolves. Stir it into the simmering chicken broth mixture and cook just until thickened.
3. Remove from heat, add salt and pepper to taste, and let cool slightly.
4. Lay biscuits out on wax paper. Peel each biscuit apart in the middle to make 2 rounds so you have 16 rounds total. Using your hands or a rolling pin, flatten each biscuit round slightly to make it larger and thinner.
5. Divide chicken filling among 8 of the biscuit rounds. Place remaining biscuit rounds on top and press edges all around. Use the tines of a fork to crimp biscuit edges and make sure they are sealed well.
6. Spray both sides lightly with oil or cooking spray.
7. Cook in a single layer, 4 at a time, at 170°C for 10 minutes or until biscuit dough is cooked through and golden brown.

## Chicken Patties

**Prep time: 15 minutes | Cook time: 12 minutes | Serves 4**

| | |
|---|---|
| 450 g chicken thigh mince | ¼ teaspoon onion powder |
| 110 g shredded Mozzarella cheese | 1 large egg |
| 1 teaspoon dried parsley | 60 g pork rinds, finely ground |
| ½ teaspoon garlic powder | |

Cook:
1. In a large bowl, mix chicken mince, Mozzarella, parsley, garlic powder, and onion powder. form into four patties.
2. Place patties in the freezer for 15 to 20 minutes until they begin to firm up.
3. Whisk egg in a medium bowl. Place the ground pork rinds into a large bowl.
4. Dip each chicken patty into the egg and then press into pork rinds to fully coat. Place patties into the air fryer drawer.
5. Adjust the temperature to 180°C and air fry for 12 minutes.
6. Patties will be firm and cooked to an internal temperature of 76°C when done. Serve immediately.

## Turkish Chicken Kebabs

**Prep time: 30 minutes | Cook time: 15 minutes | Serves 4**

| | |
|---|---|
| 70 g plain Greek yogurt | 1 teaspoon sweet Hungarian paprika |
| 1 tablespoon minced garlic | ½ teaspoon ground cinnamon |
| 1 tablespoon tomato paste | ½ teaspoon black pepper |
| 1 tablespoon fresh lemon juice | ½ teaspoon cayenne pepper |
| 1 tablespoon vegetable oil | 450 g boneless, skinless chicken thighs, quartered crosswise |
| 1 teaspoon kosher salt | |
| 1 teaspoon ground cumin | |

Cook:
1. In a large bowl, combine the yogurt, garlic, tomato paste, lemon juice, vegetable oil, salt, cumin, paprika, cinnamon, black pepper, and cayenne. Stir until the spices are blended into the yogurt.
2. Add the chicken to the bowl and toss until well coated. Marinate at room temperature for 30 minutes, or cover and refrigerate for up to 24 hours.
3. Arrange the chicken in a single layer in the air fryer drawer. Set the air fryer to (190°C for 10 minutes. Turn the chicken and cook for 5 minutes more. Use a meat thermometer to ensure the chicken has reached an internal temperature of 76°C.

## Teriyaki Chicken Legs

**Prep time: 12 minutes | Cook time: 18 to 20 minutes | Serves 2**

| | |
|---|---|
| 4 tablespoons teriyaki sauce | 4 chicken legs |
| 1 tablespoon orange juice | Cooking spray |
| 1 teaspoon smoked paprika | |

Cook:

1. Mix together the teriyaki sauce, orange juice, and smoked paprika. Brush on all sides of chicken legs.
2. Spray the air fryer drawer with nonstick cooking spray and place chicken in drawer.
3. Air fry at 180ºC for 6 minutes. Turn and baste with sauce. Cook for 6 more minutes, turn and baste. Cook for 6 to 8 minutes more, until juices run clear when chicken is pierced with a fork.

## Yakitori & Crisp Paprika Chicken Drumsticks

**Prep time: 15 minutes | Cook time: 22 minutes | Serves 4-6**

### Yakitori:

| | |
|---|---|
| 120 ml mirin | 4 medium spring onions, trimmed, cut into 1½-inch pieces |
| 60 ml dry white wine | |
| 120 ml soy sauce | |
| 1 tablespoon light brown sugar | Cooking spray |
| | Special Equipment: |
| 680 g boneless, skinless chicken thighs, cut into 1½-inch pieces, fat trimmed | 4 (4-inch) bamboo skewers, soaked in water for at least 30 minutes |

### Chicken Drumsticks:

| | |
|---|---|
| 2 teaspoons paprika | Pinch pepper |
| 1 teaspoon packed brown sugar | 4 (140 g) chicken drumsticks, trimmed |
| 1 teaspoon garlic powder | 1 teaspoon vegetable oil |
| ½ teaspoon dry mustard | 1 scallion, green part only, sliced thin on bias |
| ½ teaspoon salt | |

Prep for Yakitori:

1. Combine the mirin, dry white wine, soy sauce, and brown sugar in a saucepan. Bring to a boil over medium heat. Keep stirring. 2. Boil for another 2 minutes or until it has a thick consistency. Turn off the heat. 3. Spritz the air fryer drawer in Zone One with cooking spray. 4. Run the bamboo skewers through the chicken pieces and spring onions alternatively. 5. Arrange the skewers in the set air fryer, then brush with mirin mixture on both sides. Spritz with cooking spray.

Prep for Chicken Drumstick:

1. Combine paprika, sugar, garlic powder, mustard, salt, and pepper in a bowl. Pat drumsticks dry with paper towels. Using metal skewer, poke 10 to 15 holes in skin of each drumstick. Rub with oil and sprinkle evenly with spice mixture. 2. Arrange drumsticks in air fryer drawer of Zone Two, spaced evenly apart, alternating ends.

Cook:

1. Set Zone One of air fryer to 200ºC, select Air Fry, set the cook time to 10 minutes.
2. Press MATCH, set the cook time of Zone Two to 22-25 minutes. Press SYNC, then press Start.
3. for Yakitori, cook until the chicken and spring onions are glossy. Flip the skewers halfway through. Serve immediately.
4. for chicken drumstick, air fry until chicken is crisp and registers 90ºC, flipping chicken halfway through cooking. Transfer chicken to serving platter, tent loosely with aluminum foil, and let rest for 5 minutes.

## Herb-Buttermilk Chicken Breast

**Prep time: 5 minutes | Cook time: 40 minutes | Serves 2**

| | |
|---|---|
| 1 large bone-in, skin-on chicken breast | ½ teaspoon dried dill |
| | ½ teaspoon onion powder |
| 240 ml buttermilk | ¼ teaspoon garlic powder |
| 1½ teaspoons dried parsley | ¼ teaspoon dried tarragon |
| 1½ teaspoons dried chives | Cooking spray |
| ¾ teaspoon kosher salt | |

Cook:

1. Place the chicken breast in a bowl and pour over the buttermilk, turning the chicken in it to make sure it's completely covered. Let the chicken stand at room temperature for at least 20 minutes or in the refrigerator for up to 4 hours.
2. Meanwhile, in a bowl, stir together the parsley, chives, salt, dill, onion powder, garlic powder, and tarragon.
3. Set the air fryer to 150ºC.
4. Remove the chicken from the buttermilk, letting the excess drip off, then place the chicken skin-side up directly in the air fryer. Sprinkle the seasoning mix all over the top of the chicken breast, then let stand until the herb mix soaks into the buttermilk, at least 5 minutes.
5. Spray the top of the chicken with cooking spray. Bake for 10 minutes, then increase the temperature to 180ºC and bake until an instant-read thermometer inserted into the thickest part of the breast reads 80ºC and the chicken is deep golden brown, 30

to 35 minutes.

6. Transfer the chicken breast to a cutting board, let rest for 10 minutes, then cut the meat off the bone and cut into thick slices for serving.

## One-Dish Chicken and Rice

**Prep time: 10 minutes | Cook time: 40 minutes | Serves 4**

| | |
|---|---|
| 190 g long-grain white rice, rinsed and drained | 1 tablespoon toasted sesame oil |
| 120 g cut frozen green beans (do not thaw) | 1 teaspoon kosher salt |
| | 1 teaspoon black pepper |
| 1 tablespoon minced fresh ginger | 450 g chicken wings, preferably drumettes |
| 3 cloves garlic, minced | |

Cook:

1. In a baking dish, combine the rice, green beans, ginger, garlic, sesame oil, salt, and pepper. Stir to combine. Place the chicken wings on top of the rice mixture.
2. Cover the pan with foil. Make a long slash in the foil to allow the pan to vent steam. Place the pan in the air fryer drawer. Set the air fryer to (190°C for 30 minutes.
3. Remove the foil. Set the air fryer to 200°C for 10 minutes, or until the wings have browned and rendered fat into the rice and vegetables, turning the wings halfway through the cooking time.

## French Garlic Chicken

**Prep time: 30 minutes | Cook time: 27 minutes | Serves 4**

| | |
|---|---|
| 2 tablespoon extra-virgin olive oil | ½ teaspoon kosher salt |
| | 1 teaspoon black pepper |
| 1 tablespoon Dijon mustard | 450 g boneless, skinless chicken thighs, halved crosswise |
| 1 tablespoon apple cider vinegar | |
| 3 cloves garlic, minced | 2 tablespoons butter |
| 2 teaspoons herbes de Provence | 8 cloves garlic, chopped |
| | 60 g heavy whipping cream |

Cook:

1. In a small bowl, combine the olive oil, mustard, vinegar, minced garlic, herbes de Provence, salt, and pepper. Use a wire whisk to emulsify the mixture.
2. Pierce the chicken all over with a fork to allow the marinade to penetrate better. Place the chicken in a resealable plastic bag, pour the marinade over, and seal. Massage until the chicken is well coated. Marinate at room temperature for 30 minutes or in the refrigerator for up to 24 hours.
3. When you are ready to cook, place the butter and chopped garlic in a baking dish and place it in the air fryer drawer. Set the air fryer to 200°C for 5 minutes, or until the butter has melted and the garlic is sizzling.
4. Add the chicken and the marinade to the seasoned butter. Set the air fryer to 180°C for 15 minutes. Use a meat thermometer to ensure the chicken has reached an internal temperature of 76°C. Transfer the chicken to a plate and cover lightly with foil to keep warm.
5. Add the cream to the pan, stirring to combine with the garlic, butter, and cooking juices. Place the pan in the air fryer drawer. Set the air fryer to 180°C for 7 minutes.
6. Pour the thickened sauce over the chicken and serve.

## Thai Tacos with Peanut Sauce

**Prep time: 10 minutes | Cook time: 6 minutes | Serves 4**

| | |
|---|---|
| 450 g chicken mince | 2 tablespoons wheat-free tamari or coconut aminos |
| 10 g diced onions (about 1 small onion) | |
| | 1½ teaspoons hot sauce |
| 2 cloves garlic, minced | 5 drops liquid stevia (optional) |
| ¼ teaspoon fine sea salt | |
| Sauce: | for Serving: |
| 60 g creamy peanut butter, room temperature | 2 small heads butter lettuce, leaves separated |
| 2 tablespoons chicken broth, plus more if needed | Lime slices (optional) |
| | for Garnish (Optional): |
| 2 tablespoons lime juice | Coriander leaves |
| 2 tablespoons grated fresh ginger | Shredded purple cabbage |
| | Sliced green onions |

Cook:

1. Set the air fryer to 180°C.
2. Place the chicken mince, onions, garlic, and salt in a pie pan or a dish that will fit in your air fryer. Break up the chicken with a spatula. Place in the air fryer and bake for 5 minutes, or until the chicken is browned and cooked through. Break up the chicken again into small crumbles.
3. Make the sauce: In a medium-sized bowl, stir together the peanut butter, broth, lime juice, ginger, tamari, hot sauce, and stevia (if using) until well combined. If the sauce is too thick, add another tablespoon or two of broth. Taste and add more hot sauce if desired.
4. Add half of the sauce to the pan with the chicken. Cook for another minute, until heated through, and stir well to combine.
5. Assemble the tacos: Place several lettuce leaves on a servin plate. Place a few tablespoons of the chicken mixture in ea

lettuce leaf and garnish with coriander leaves, purple cabbage, and sliced green onions, if desired. Serve the remaining sauce on the side. Serve with lime slices, if desired.
6. Store leftover meat mixture in an airtight container in the refrigerator for up to 4 days; store leftover sauce, lettuce leaves, and garnishes separately. Reheat the meat mixture in a lightly greased pie pan in a set 180°C air fryer for 3 minutes, or until heated through.

## Chicken Drumsticks with Barbecue-Honey Sauce

**Prep time: 5 minutes | Cook time: 40 minutes | Serves 5**

| | |
|---|---|
| 1 tablespoon olive oil | Salt and ground black pepper, to taste |
| 10 chicken drumsticks | 240 ml barbecue sauce |
| Chicken seasoning or rub, to taste | 85 g honey |

Cook:
1. Set the air fryer to 200°C. Grease the air fryer drawer with olive oil.
2. Rub the chicken drumsticks with chicken seasoning or rub, salt and ground black pepper on a clean work surface.
3. Arrange the chicken drumsticks in a single layer in the air fryer, then air fry for 18 minutes or until lightly browned. Flip the drumsticks halfway through. You may need to work in batches to avoid overcrowding.
4. Meanwhile, combine the barbecue sauce and honey in a small bowl. Stir to mix well.
5. Remove the drumsticks from the air fryer and baste with the sauce mixture to serve.

## Italian Flavour Chicken Breasts with Roma Tomatoes

**Prep time: 10 minutes | Cook time: 60 minutes | Serves 8**

| | |
|---|---|
| 1.4 kg chicken breasts, bone-in | 1 teaspoon cayenne pepper |
| 1 teaspoon minced fresh basil | ½ teaspoon salt |
| 1 teaspoon minced fresh rosemary | ½ teaspoon freshly ground black pepper |
| 2 tablespoons minced fresh parsley | 4 medium Roma tomatoes, halved |
| | Cooking spray |

Cook:

1. Set the air fryer to 190°C. Spritz the air fryer drawer with cooking spray.
2. Combine all the ingredients, except for the chicken breasts and tomatoes, in a large bowl. Stir to mix well.
3. Dunk the chicken breasts in the mixture and press to coat well.
4. Transfer the chicken breasts in the set air fryer. You may need to work in batches to avoid overcrowding.
5. Air fry for 25 minutes or until the internal temperature of the thickest part of the breasts reaches at least 76°C. Flip the breasts halfway through the cooking time.
6. Remove the cooked chicken breasts from the drawer and adjust the temperature to 180°C.
7. Place the tomatoes in the air fryer and spritz with cooking spray. Sprinkle with a touch of salt and cook for 10 minutes or until tender. Shake the drawer halfway through the cooking time.
8. Serve the tomatoes with chicken breasts on a large serving plate.

## Celery Chicken & Spicy Chicken Thighs and Gold Potatoes

**Prep time: 15 minutes | Cook time: 25 minutes | Serves 4-6**

**Celery Chicken:**

| | |
|---|---|
| 120 ml soy sauce | tenderloins |
| 2 tablespoons hoisin sauce | 120 g chopped celery |
| 4 teaspoons minced garlic | 1 medium red bell pepper, diced |
| 1 teaspoon freshly ground black pepper | Olive oil spray |
| 8 boneless, skinless chicken | |

**Spicy Chicken Thighs and Gold Potatoes:**

| | |
|---|---|
| 4 bone-in, skin-on chicken thighs | leaves |
| ½ teaspoon kosher salt or ¼ teaspoon fine salt | ½ teaspoon dry mustard |
| | ½ teaspoon granulated garlic |
| 2 tablespoons melted unsalted butter | ¼ teaspoon paprika |
| | ¼ teaspoon hot pepper sauce |
| 2 teaspoons Worcestershire sauce | Cooking oil spray |
| | 4 medium Yukon gold potatoes, chopped |
| 2 teaspoons curry powder | 1 tablespoon extra-virgin olive oil |
| 1 teaspoon dried oregano | |

Prep for Celery Chicken:
1. Spray the air fryer drawer of Zone One lightly with olive oil spray. 2. In a large bowl, mix together the soy sauce, hoisin sauce, garlic, and black pepper to make a marinade. Add the chicken, celery, and bell pepper and toss to coat. 3. Shake the

excess marinade off the chicken, place it and the vegetables in the air fryer drawer, and lightly spray with olive oil spray. Reserve the remaining marinade.

Prep for Spicy Chicken Thighs and Gold Potatoes:
1. Sprinkle the chicken thighs on both sides with salt. 2. In a medium bowl, stir together the melted butter, Worcestershire sauce, curry powder, oregano, dry mustard, granulated garlic, paprika, and hot pepper sauce. Add the thighs to the sauce and stir to coat. Spray the crisper plate with cooking oil. In the drawer, combine the potatoes and olive oil and toss to coat. Add the wire rack to the air fryer and place the chicken thighs on top. 3. Insert the crisper plate into the drawer and the drawer into the Zone Two.

Cook:
1. Set Zone One of the air fryer to 190°C, select Air Fry, select the cook time to 8 minutes. 2. Press MATCH, set the temperature of Zone Two to 200°C, and set the time to 25 minutes.
3. Press SYNC, then press START.
4. for celery chicken, turn the chicken over and brush with some of the remaining marinade. Air fry for an additional 5 to 7 minutes, or until the chicken reaches an internal temperature of at least 76°C. Serve.
5. for Spicy Chicken Thighs and Gold Potatoes, after 19 minutes, check the chicken thighs. If a food thermometer inserted into the chicken registers 76°C, transfer them to a clean plate, and cover with aluminum foil to keep warm. If they aren't cooked to 76°C, resume cooking for another 1 to 2 minutes until they are done. Remove them from the unit along with the rack. Remove the drawer and shake it to distribute the potatoes. Reinsert the drawer to resume cooking for 3 to 6 minutes, or until the potatoes are crisp and golden brown. When the cooking is complete, serve the chicken with the potatoes.

## Blackened Cajun Chicken Tenders

**Prep time: 10 minutes | Cook time: 17 minutes | Serves 4**

| | |
|---|---|
| 2 teaspoons paprika | pepper |
| 1 teaspoon chili powder | 2 tablespoons coconut oil |
| ½ teaspoon garlic powder | 450 g boneless, skinless chicken tenders |
| ½ teaspoon dried thyme | 60 ml full-fat ranch dressing |
| ¼ teaspoon onion powder | |
| ⅛ teaspoon ground cayenne | |

Cook:
1. In a small bowl, combine all seasonings.
2. Drizzle oil over chicken tenders and then generously coat each tender in the spice mixture. Place tenders into the air fryer drawer.
3. Adjust the temperature to (190°C and air fry for 17 minutes.
4. Tenders will be 76°C internally when fully cooked. Serve with ranch dressing for dipping.

## Pork Rind Fried Chicken

**Prep time: 30 minutes | Cook time: 20 minutes | Serves 4**

| | |
|---|---|
| 60 ml buffalo sauce | ¼ teaspoon ground black pepper |
| 4 (115 g) boneless, skinless chicken breasts | 60 g g plain pork rinds, finely crushed |
| ½ teaspoon paprika | |
| ½ teaspoon garlic powder | |

Cook:
1. Pour buffalo sauce into a large sealable bowl or bag. Add chicken and toss to coat. Place sealed bowl or bag into refrigerator and let marinate at least 30 minutes up to overnight.
2. Remove chicken from marinade but do not shake excess sauce off chicken. Sprinkle both sides of thighs with paprika, garlic powder, and pepper.
3. Place pork rinds into a large bowl and press each chicken breast into pork rinds to coat evenly on both sides.
4. Place chicken into ungreased air fryer drawer. Adjust the temperature to 200°C and roast for 20 minutes, turning chicken halfway through cooking. Chicken will be golden and have an internal temperature of at least 76°C when done. Serve warm.

## Nashville Hot Chicken

**Prep time: 20 minutes | Cook time: 24 to 28 minutes | Serves 8**

| | |
|---|---|
| 1.4 kg bone-in, skin-on chicken pieces, breasts halved crosswise | divided |
| | 120 g heavy (whipping) cream |
| 1 tablespoon sea salt | 2 large eggs, beaten |
| 1 tablespoon freshly ground black pepper | 1 tablespoon vinegar-based hot sauce |
| 70 g finely ground blanched almond flour | Avocado oil spray |
| | 115 g unsalted butter |
| 130 g grated Parmesan cheese | 120 ml avocado oil |
| 1 tablespoon baking powder | 1 tablespoon cayenne pepper (more or less to taste) |
| 2 teaspoons garlic powder, | 2 tablespoons Xylitol |

Cook:
1. Sprinkle the chicken with the salt and pepper.

Chapter 4  Poultry  | 27

2. In a large shallow bowl, whisk together the almond flour, Parmesan cheese, baking powder, and 1 teaspoon of the garlic powder.
3. In a separate bowl, whisk together the heavy cream, eggs, and hot sauce.
4. Dip the chicken pieces in the egg, then coat each with the almond flour mixture, pressing the mixture into the chicken to adhere. Allow to sit for 15 minutes to let the breading set.
5. Set the air fryer to 200ºC. Place the chicken in a single layer in the air fryer drawer, being careful not to overcrowd the pieces, working in batches if necessary. Spray the chicken with oil and roast for 13 minutes.
6. Carefully flip the chicken and spray it with more oil. Reduce the air fryer temperature to 180ºC. Roast for another 11 to 15 minutes, until an instant-read thermometer reads 70ºC.
7. While the chicken cooks, heat the butter, avocado oil, cayenne pepper, xylitol, and remaining 1 teaspoon of garlic powder in a saucepan over medium-low heat. Cook until the butter is melted and the sugar substitute has dissolved.
8. Remove the chicken from the air fryer. Use tongs to dip the chicken in the sauce. Place the coated chicken on a rack over a baking sheet, and allow it to rest for 5 minutes before serving.

## Chicken Schnitzel Dogs

**Prep time: 15 minutes | Cook time: 8 to 10 minutes | Serves 4**

| | |
|---|---|
| 30 g flour | thin |
| ½ teaspoon salt | Oil for misting or cooking spray |
| 1 teaspoon marjoram | 4 whole-grain hotdog buns |
| 1 teaspoon dried parsley flakes | 4 slices Gouda cheese |
| ½ teaspoon thyme | 1 small Granny Smith apple, thinly sliced |
| 1 egg | 45 g shredded Swiss Chard cabbage |
| 1 teaspoon lemon juice | Coleslaw dressing |
| 1 teaspoon water | |
| 60 g bread crumbs | |
| 4 chicken tenders, pounded | |

**Cook:**
1. In a shallow dish, mix together the flour, salt, marjoram, parsley, and thyme.
2. In another shallow dish, beat together egg, lemon juice, and water.
3. Place bread crumbs in a third shallow dish.
4. Cut each of the flattened chicken tenders in half lengthwise.
5. Dip flattened chicken strips in flour mixture, then egg wash. Let excess egg drip off and roll in bread crumbs. Spray both sides with oil or cooking spray.
6. Air fry at 200ºC for 5 minutes. Spray with oil, turn over, and spray other side.
7. Cook for 3 to 5 minutes more, until well done and crispy brown.
8. To serve, place 2 schnitzel strips on bottom of each hotdog bun. Top with cheese, sliced apple, and cabbage. Drizzle with coleslaw dressing and top with other half of bun.

## Butter and Bacon Chicken

**Prep time: 10 minutes | Cook time: 65 minutes | Serves 6**

| | |
|---|---|
| 1 (1.8 kg) whole chicken | 1 teaspoon salt |
| 2 tablespoons salted butter, softened | ½ teaspoon ground black pepper |
| 1 teaspoon dried thyme | 6 slices sugar-free bacon |
| ½ teaspoon garlic powder | |

**Cook:**
1. Pat chicken dry with a paper towel, then rub with butter on all sides. Sprinkle thyme, garlic powder, salt, and pepper over chicken.
2. Place chicken into ungreased air fryer drawer, breast side up. Lay strips of bacon over chicken and secure with toothpicks.
3. Adjust the temperature to 180ºC and air fry for 65 minutes. Halfway through cooking, remove and set aside bacon and flip chicken over. Chicken will be done when the skin is golden and crispy and the internal temperature is at least 76ºC. Serve warm with bacon.

## Broccoli and Cheese Stuffed Chicken

**Prep time: 15 minutes | Cook time: 20 minutes | Serves 4**

| | |
|---|---|
| 60 g cream cheese, softened | chicken breasts |
| 70 g chopped fresh broccoli, steamed | 2 tablespoons mayonnaise |
| | ¼ teaspoon salt |
| 120 g shredded sharp Cheddar cheese | ¼ teaspoon garlic powder |
| | ⅛ teaspoon ground black pepper |
| 4 (170 g) boneless, skinless | |

**Cook:**
1. In a medium bowl, combine cream cheese, broccoli, and Cheddar. Cut a 4-inch pocket into each chicken breast. Evenly divide mixture between chicken breasts; stuff the pocket of each chicken breast with the mixture.
2. Spread ¼ tablespoon mayonnaise per side of each chicken breast, then sprinkle both sides of breasts with salt, garlic powder, and pepper.
3. Place stuffed chicken breasts into ungreased air fryer drawer

so that the open seams face up. Adjust the temperature to 180°C and air fry for 20 minutes, turning chicken halfway through cooking. When done, chicken will be golden and have an internal temperature of at least 76°C. Serve warm.

## Potato-Crusted Chicken

**Prep time: 15 minutes | Cook time: 22 to 25 minutes | Serves 4**

- 60 g buttermilk
- 1 large egg, beaten
- 180 g instant potato flakes
- 20 g grated Parmesan cheese
- 1 teaspoon salt
- ½ teaspoon freshly ground black pepper
- 2 whole boneless, skinless chicken breasts (about 450 g each), halved
- 1 to 2 tablespoons oil

Cook:

1. In a shallow bowl, whisk the buttermilk and egg until blended. In another shallow bowl, stir together the potato flakes, cheese, salt, and pepper.
2. One at a time, dip the chicken pieces in the buttermilk mixture and the potato flake mixture, coating thoroughly.
3. Set the air fryer to 200°C. Line the air fryer drawer with parchment paper.
4. Place the coated chicken on the parchment and spritz with oil.
5. Cook for 15 minutes. Flip the chicken, spritz it with oil, and cook for 7 to 10 minutes more until the outside is crispy and the inside is no longer pink.

# Chapter 5  Beef, Pork, and Lamb

## Spice-Rubbed Pork Loin

**Prep time: 5 minutes | Cook time: 20 minutes | Serves 6**

| | |
|---|---|
| 1 teaspoon paprika | 1 (680 g) boneless pork loin |
| ½ teaspoon ground cumin | ½ teaspoon salt |
| ½ teaspoon chili powder | ¼ teaspoon ground black pepper |
| ½ teaspoon garlic powder | |
| 2 tablespoons coconut oil | |

Cook:

1. In a small bowl, mix paprika, cumin, chili powder, and garlic powder.
2. Drizzle coconut oil over pork. Sprinkle pork loin with salt and pepper, then rub spice mixture evenly on all sides.
3. Place pork loin into ungreased air fryer drawer. Adjust the temperature to 200°C and air fry for 20 minutes, turning pork halfway through cooking. Pork loin will be browned and have an internal temperature of at least 64°C when done. Serve warm.

## Blue Cheese Steak Salad

**Prep time: 30 minutes | Cook time: 22 minutes | Serves 4**

| | |
|---|---|
| 2 tablespoons balsamic vinegar | 180 ml extra-virgin olive oil |
| 2 tablespoons red wine vinegar | 450 g boneless rump steak |
| 1 tablespoon Dijon mustard | Avocado oil spray |
| 1 tablespoon granulated sweetener | 1 small red onion, cut into ¼-inch-thick rounds |
| 1 teaspoon minced garlic | 170 g baby spinach |
| Sea salt and freshly ground black pepper, to taste | 120 g cherry tomatoes, halved |
| | 85 g blue cheese, crumbled |

Cook:

1. In a blender, combine the balsamic vinegar, red wine vinegar, Dijon mustard, sweetener, and garlic. Season with salt and pepper and process until smooth. With the blender running, drizzle in the olive oil. Process until well combined. Transfer to a jar with a tight-fitting lid, and refrigerate until ready to serve (it will keep for up to 2 weeks).
2. Season the steak with salt and pepper and let sit at room temperature for at least 45 minutes, time permitting.
3. Set the air fryer to 200°C. Spray the steak with oil and place it in the air fryer drawer. Air fry for 6 minutes. Flip the steak and spray it with more oil. Air fry for 6 minutes more for medium-rare or until the steak is done to your liking.
4. Transfer the steak to a plate, tent with a piece of aluminum foil, and allow it to rest.
5. Spray the onion slices with oil and place them in the air fryer drawer. Cook at 200°C for 5 minutes. Flip the onion slices and spray them with more oil. Air fry for 5 minutes more.
6. Slice the steak diagonally into thin strips. Place the spinach, cherry tomatoes, onion slices, and steak in a large bowl. Toss with the desired amount of dressing. Sprinkle with crumbled blue cheese and serve.

## Vietnamese Grilled Pork

**Prep time: 30 minutes | Cook time: 20 minutes | Serves 6**

| | |
|---|---|
| 60 g minced brown onion | ½ teaspoon black pepper |
| 2 tablespoons sugar | 680 g boneless pork shoulder, cut into ½-inch-thick slices |
| 2 tablespoons vegetable oil | 60 g chopped salted roasted peanuts |
| 1 tablespoon minced garlic | 2 tablespoons chopped fresh coriander or parsley |
| 1 tablespoon fish sauce | |
| 1 tablespoon minced fresh lemongrass | |
| 2 teaspoons dark soy sauce | |

Cook:

1. In a large bowl, combine the onion, sugar, vegetable oil, garlic, fish sauce, lemongrass, soy sauce, and pepper. Add the pork and toss to coat. Marinate at room temperature for 30 minutes, or cover and refrigerate for up to 24 hours.
2. Arrange the pork slices in the air fryer drawer; discard the marinade. Set the air fryer to 200°C for 20 minutes, turning the pork halfway through the cooking time.
3. Transfer the pork to a serving platter. Sprinkle with the peanuts and coriander and serve.

## Steak, Broccoli, and Mushroom Rice Bowls

**Prep time: 10 minutes | Cook time: 15 to 18 minutes | Serves 4**

| | |
|---|---|
| 2 tablespoons cornflour | 1 onion, chopped |
| 120 ml low-sodium beef stock | 235 g sliced white or chestnut mushrooms |
| 1 teaspoon reduced-salt soy sauce | 1 tablespoon grated peeled fresh ginger |
| 340 g rump steak, cut into 1-inch cubes | Cooked brown rice (optional), for serving |
| 120 g broccoli florets | |

Cook:

1. In a medium bowl, stir together the cornflour, beef stock, and

soy sauce until the cornflour is completely dissolved.
2. Add the beef cubes and toss to coat. Let stand for 5 minutes at room temperature.
3. Insert the crisper plate into the drawer and the drawer into the unit. Set the unit by selecting AIR FRY, setting the temperature to 200ºC, and setting the time to 3 minutes. Select START/STOP to begin.
4. Once the unit is set, use a slotted spoon to transfer the beef from the stock mixture into a medium metal bowl that fits into the drawer. Reserve the stock. Add the broccoli, onion, mushrooms, and ginger to the beef. Place the bowl into the drawer.
5. Select AIR FRY, set the temperature to 200ºC, and set the time to 18 minutes. Select START/STOP to begin.
6. After about 12 minutes, check the beef and broccoli. If a food thermometer inserted into the beef registers at least 64ºC and the vegetables are tender, add the reserved stock and resume cooking for about 3 minutes until the sauce boils. If not, resume cooking for about 3 minutes before adding the reservedstock.
7. When the cooking is complete, serve immediately over hot cooked brown rice, if desired.

## Pepper Steak

**Prep time: 30 minutes | Cook time: 16 to 20 minutes | Serves 4**

| | |
|---|---|
| 450 g minute steak, cut into 1-inch pieces | black pepper |
| 235 ml Italian dressing | 30 g cornflour |
| 355 ml beef stock | 235 g thinly sliced pepper, any color |
| 1 tablespoon soy sauce | 235 g chopped celery |
| ½ teaspoon salt | 1 tablespoon minced garlic |
| ¼ teaspoon freshly ground | 1 to 2 tablespoons oil |

Cook:
1. In a large resealable bag, combine the beef and Italian dressing. Seal the bag and refrigerate to marinate for 8 hours.
2. In a small bowl, whisk the beef stock, soy sauce, salt, and pepper until blended.
3. In another small bowl, whisk 60 ml water and the cornflour until dissolved. Stir the cornflour mixture into the beef stock mixture until blended.
4. Set the air fryer to 190ºC.
5. Pour the stock mixture into a baking tray. Cook for 4 minutes. Stir and cook for 4 to 5 minutes more. Remove and set aside.
6. Increase the air fryer temperature to 200ºC. Line the air fryer drawer with parchment paper.
7. Remove the steak from the marinade and place it in a medium bowl. Discard the marinade. Stir in the pepper, celery, and garlic.
8. Place the steak and pepper mixture on the parchment. Spritz with oil.
9. Cook for 4 minutes. Shake the drawer and cook for 4 to 7 minutes more, until the vegetables are tender and the meat reaches an internal temperature of 64ºC. Serve with the gravy.

## Mustard Lamb Chops

**Prep time: 5 minutes | Cook time: 14 minutes | Serves 4**

| | |
|---|---|
| Oil, for spraying | ¼ teaspoon freshly ground black pepper |
| 1 tablespoon Dijon mustard | 4 (1¼-inch-thick) loin lamb chops |
| 2 teaspoons lemon juice | |
| ½ teaspoon dried tarragon | |
| ¼ teaspoon salt | |

Cook:
1. Set the air fryer to 200ºC. Line the air fryer drawer with parchment and spray lightly with oil.
2. In a small bowl, mix together the mustard, lemon juice, tarragon, salt, and black pepper.
3. Pat dry the lamb chops with a paper towel. Brush the chops on both sides with the mustard mixture.
4. Place the chops in the prepared drawer. You may need to work in batches, depending on the size of your air fryer.
5. Cook for 8 minutes, flip, and cook for another 6 minutes, or until the internal temperature reaches 52ºC for rare, 64ºC for medium-rare, or 68ºC for medium.

## Pork Shoulder with Garlicky Coriander-Parsley Sauce

**Prep time: 1 hour 15 minutes | Cook time: 30 minutes | Serves 4**

| | |
|---|---|
| 1 teaspoon flaxseed meal | pepper, to taste |
| 1 egg white, well whisked | Garlicky Coriander-Parsley Sauce: |
| 1 tablespoon soy sauce | |
| 1 teaspoon lemon juice, preferably freshly squeezed | 3 garlic cloves, minced |
| | 80 g fresh coriander leaves |
| 1 tablespoon olive oil | 80 g fresh parsley leaves |
| 450 g pork shoulder, cut into pieces 2-inches long | 1 teaspoon lemon juice |
| | ½ tablespoon salt |
| Salt and ground black | 80 ml extra-virgin olive oi |

Cook:
1. Combine the flaxseed meal, egg white, soy sauce, lemon juice, salt, black pepper, and olive oil in a large bowl. Dunk the pork strips in and press to submerge.

2. Wrap the bowl in plastic and refrigerate to marinate for at least an hour.
3. Set the air fryer to 190ºC.
4. Arrange the marinated pork strips in the set air fryer and air fry for 30 minutes or until cooked through and well browned. Flip the strips halfway through.
5. Meanwhile, combine the ingredients for the sauce in a small bowl. Stir to mix well. Arrange the bowl in the refrigerator to chill until ready to serve.
6. Serve the air fried pork strips with the chilled sauce.

## Pork Loin Roast

### Prep time: 30 minutes | Cook time: 55 minutes | Serves 6

| | |
|---|---|
| 680 g boneless pork loin joint, washed | ¾ teaspoon sea salt flakes |
| 1 teaspoon mustard seeds | 1 teaspoon red pepper flakes, crushed |
| 1 teaspoon garlic powder | 2 dried sprigs thyme, crushed |
| 1 teaspoon porcini powder | 2 tablespoons lime juice |
| 1 teaspoon onion granules | |

Cook:
1. Firstly, score the meat using a small knife; make sure to not cut too deep.
2. In a small-sized mixing dish, combine all seasonings in the order listed above; mix to combine well.
3. Massage the spice mix into the pork meat to evenly distribute. Drizzle with lemon juice.
4. Set the air fryer to 180ºC. Place the pork in the air fryer drawer; roast for 25 to 30 minutes. Pause the machine, check for doneness and cook for 25 minutes more.

## Herbed Lamb Steaks

### Prep time: 30 minutes | Cook time: 15 minutes | Serves 4

| | |
|---|---|
| ½ medium onion | 1 teaspoon cayenne pepper |
| 2 tablespoons minced garlic | 1 teaspoon salt |
| 2 teaspoons ground ginger | 4 (170 g) boneless lamb sirloin steaks |
| 1 teaspoon ground cinnamon | Oil, for spraying |
| 1 teaspoon onion granules | |

Cook:
1. In a blender, combine the onion, garlic, ginger, cinnamon, onion granules, cayenne pepper, and salt and pulse until the onion is minced.
2. Place the lamb steaks in a large bowl or zip-top plastic bag and sprinkle the onion mixture over the top. Turn the steaks until they are evenly coated. Cover with plastic wrap or seal the bag and refrigerate for 30 minutes.
3. Set the air fryer to 160ºC. Line the air fryer drawer with parchment and spray lightly with oil.
4. Place the lamb steaks in a single layer in the prepared drawer, making sure they don't overlap. You may need to work in batches, depending on the size of your air fryer.
5. Cook for 8 minutes, flip, and cook for another 7 minutes, or until the internal temperature reaches 68ºC.

## Pork Kebab with Yogurt Sauce & Beef Mince Taco Rolls

### Prep time: 45 minutes | Cook time: 12 minutes | Serves 4-6

#### Pork Kebab:

| | |
|---|---|
| 2 teaspoons olive oil | ½ teaspoon celery salt |
| 230 g pork mince | Yogurt Sauce: |
| 230 g beef mince | 2 tablespoons olive oil |
| 1 egg, whisked | 2 tablespoons fresh lemon juice |
| Sea salt and ground black pepper, to taste | Sea salt, to taste |
| 1 teaspoon paprika | ¼ teaspoon red pepper flakes, crushed |
| 2 garlic cloves, minced | 120 ml full-fat yogurt |
| 1 teaspoon dried marjoram | 1 teaspoon dried dill |
| 1 teaspoon mustard seeds | |

#### Taco Rolls:

| | |
|---|---|
| 230 g 80/20 beef mince | coriander |
| 80 ml water | 355 g shredded Mozzarella cheese |
| 1 tablespoon chili powder | 60 g blanched finely ground almond flour |
| 2 teaspoons cumin | 60 g full-fat cream cheese |
| ½ teaspoon garlic powder | 1 large egg |
| ¼ teaspoon dried oregano | |
| 60 g tinned diced tomatoes | |
| 2 tablespoons chopped | |

Prep for Pork Kebab:
1. Spritz the sides and bottom of the air fryer drawer with 2 teaspoons of olive oil. 2. In a mixing dish, thoroughly combine the pork, beef, egg, salt, black pepper, paprika, garlic, marjoram, mustard seeds, and celery salt. 3. form the mixture into kebabs and transfer them to the greased drawer in Zone One.

Prep for Taco Rolls:
1. In a medium skillet over medium heat, brown the beef mince about 7 to 10 minutes. When meat is fully cooked, drain. 2. Add water to skillet and stir in chili powder, cumin, garlic powder, oregano, and tomatoes. Add coriander. Bring to a boil, then

reduce heat to simmer for 3 minutes. 3. In a large microwave-safe bowl, place Mozzarella, almond flour, cream cheese, and egg. Microwave for 1 minute. Stir the mixture quickly until smooth ball of dough forms. 4. Cut a piece of parchment for your work surface. Press the dough into a large rectangle on the parchment, wetting your hands to prevent the dough from sticking as necessary. Cut the dough into eight rectangles. 5. On each rectangle place a few spoons of the meat mixture. Fold the short ends of each roll toward the center and roll the length as you would a burrito. 6. Cut a piece of parchment to fit your air fryer drawer. Place taco rolls onto the parchment and place into the air fryer drawer of Zone Two.

Cook:

1. Set the Zone One to 190ºC, select air fry, set the cook time to 12 minutes.
2. Press MATCH, set the Zone Two to 180ºC, set the cook time to 10 minutes.
3. Press SYNC, then press START.
4. for Pork Kebab, turning them over once or twice. In the meantime, mix all the sauce ingredients and place in the refrigerator until ready to serve. Serve the pork kebabs with the yogurt sauce on the side.
2. for Taco Rolls, flip halfway through the cooking time. Allow to cool 10 minutes before serving.

## Five-Spice Pork Belly

**Prep time: 10 minutes | Cook time: 17 minutes | Serves 4**

| | |
|---|---|
| 450 g unsalted pork belly | 120 ml beef or chicken stock |
| 2 teaspoons Chinese five-spice powder | ¼ to 120 ml liquid or powdered sweetener |
| Sauce: | 3 tablespoons wheat-free tamari |
| 1 tablespoon coconut oil | |
| 1 (1-inch) piece fresh ginger, peeled and grated | 1 spring onion, sliced, plus more for garnish |
| 2 cloves garlic, minced | |

Cook:

1. Spray the air fryer drawer with avocado oil. Set the air fryer to 200ºC.
2. Cut the pork belly into ½-inch-thick slices and season well on all sides with the five-spice powder. Place the slices in a single layer in the air fryer drawer (if you're using a smaller air fryer, work in batches if necessary) and cook for 8 minutes, or until cooked to your liking, flipping halfway through.
3. While the pork belly cooks, make the sauce: Heat the coconut oil in a small saucepan over medium heat. Add the ginger and garlic and sauté for 1 minute, or until fragrant.

Add the stock, sweetener, and tamari and simmer for 10 to 15 minutes, until thickened. Add the spring onion and cook for another minute, until the spring onion is softened. Taste and adjust the seasoning to your liking.

4. Transfer the pork belly to a large bowl. Pour the sauce over the pork belly and coat well. Place the pork belly slices on a serving platter and garnish with sliced spring onions.
5. Best served fresh. Store leftovers in an airtight container in the fridge for up to 4 days. Reheat in a set 200ºC air fryer for 3 minutes, or until heated through.

## Air Fried Crispy Venison

**Prep time: 10 minutes | Cook time: 20 minutes | Serves 4**

| | |
|---|---|
| 2 eggs | pepper |
| 60 ml milk | 450 g venison backstrap/striploin, sliced |
| 120 g whole wheat flour | Cooking spray |
| ½ teaspoon salt | |
| ¼ teaspoon ground black | |

Cook:

1. Set the air fryer to 180ºC and spritz with cooking spray.
2. Whisk the eggs with milk in a large bowl. Combine the flour with salt and ground black pepper in a shallow dish.
3. Dredge the venison in the flour first, then into the egg mixture. Shake the excess off and roll the venison back over the flour to coat well.
4. Arrange half of the venison in the set air fryer and spritz with cooking spray.
5. Air fry for 10 minutes or until the internal temperature of the venison reaches at least 64ºC for medium rare. Flip the venison halfway through. Repeat with remaining venison.
6. Serve immediately.

## Italian Sausages with Peppers and Onions

**Prep time: 5 minutes | Cook time: 28 minutes | Serves 3**

| | |
|---|---|
| 1 medium onion, thinly sliced | coconut oil |
| 1 yellow or orange pepper, thinly sliced | 1 teaspoon fine sea salt |
| | 6 Italian-seasoned sausages |
| 1 red pepper, thinly sliced | Dijon mustard, for serving (optional) |
| 60 ml avocado oil or melted | |

Cook:

1. Set the air fryer to 200ºC.
2. Place the onion and peppers in a large bowl. Drizzle with the

oil and toss well to coat the veggies. Season with the salt.

3. Place the onion and peppers in a pie pan and cook in the air fryer for 8 minutes, stirring halfway through. Remove from the air fryer and set aside.

4. Spray the air fryer drawer with avocado oil. Place the sausages in the air fryer drawer and air fry for 20 minutes, or until crispy and golden brown. During the last minute or two of cooking, add the onion and peppers to the drawer with the sausages to warm them through.

5. Place the onion and peppers on a serving platter and arrange the sausages on top. Serve Dijon mustard on the side, if desired.

6. Store leftovers in an airtight container in the fridge for up to 7 days or in the freezer for up to a month. Reheat in a set 200ºC air fryer for 3 minutes, or until heated through.

## Bulgogi Burgers

**Prep time: 30 minutes | Cook time: 10 minutes | Serves 4**

| Burgers: | ½ teaspoon coarse or flaky |
| 450 g 85% lean beef mince | salt |
| 60 g chopped spring onionspring onions | Gochujang Mayonnaise: |
| 2 tablespoons gochujang (Korean red chili paste) | 60 ml mayonnaise |
| 1 tablespoon dark soy sauce | 60 g chopped spring onionspring onions |
| 2 teaspoons minced garlic | 1 tablespoon gochujang (Korean red chili paste) |
| 2 teaspoons minced fresh ginger | 1 tablespoon toasted sesame oil |
| 2 teaspoons sugar | 2 teaspoons sesame seeds |
| 1 tablespoon toasted sesame oil | 4 hamburger buns |

Cook:

1. for the burgers: In a large bowl, mix the ground beef, spring onionspring onions, gochujang, soy sauce, garlic, ginger, sugar, sesame oil, and salt. Marinate at room temperature for 30 minutes, or cover and refrigerate for up to 24 hours.

2. Divide the meat into four portions and form them into round patties. Make a slight depression in the middle of each patty with your thumb to prevent them from puffing up into a dome shape while cooking.

3. Place the patties in a single layer in the air fryer drawer. Set the air fryer to 180ºC for 10 minutes.

4. Meanwhile, for the gochujang mayonnaise: Stir together the mayonnaise, spring onionspring onions, gochujang, sesame oil, and sesame seeds.

5. At the end of the cooking time, use a meat thermometer to ensure the burgers have reached an internal temperature of 72ºC (medium).

6. To serve, place the burgers on the buns and top with the mayonnaise.

## Steak with Bell Pepper

**Prep time: 30 minutes | Cook time: 20 to 23 minutes | Serves 6**

| 60 ml avocado oil | bavette or skirt steak, thinly sliced against the grain |
| 60 g freshly squeezed lime juice | 1 red pepper, cored, seeded, and cut into ½-inch slices |
| 2 teaspoons minced garlic | 1 green pepper, cored, seeded, and cut into ½-inch slices |
| 1 tablespoon chili powder | |
| ½ teaspoon ground cumin | |
| Sea salt and freshly ground black pepper, to taste | 1 large onion, sliced |
| 450 g top rump steak or | |

Cook:

1. In a small bowl or blender, combine the avocado oil, lime juice, garlic, chili powder, cumin, and salt and pepper to taste.

2. Place the sliced steak in a zip-top bag or shallow dish. Place the peppers and onion in a separate zip-top bag or dish. Pour half the marinade over the steak and the other half over the vegetables. Seal both bags and let the steak and vegetables marinate in the refrigerator for at least 1 hour or up to 4 hours.

3. Line the air fryer drawer with an air fryer liner or aluminum foil. Remove the vegetables from their bag or dish and shake off any excess marinade. Set the air fryer to 200ºC. Place the vegetables in the air fryer drawer and cook for 13 minutes.

4. Remove the steak from its bag or dish and shake off any excess marinade. Place the steak on top of the vegetables in the air fryer, and cook for 7 to 10 minutes or until an instant-read thermometer reads 49ºC for medium-rare (or cook to your desired doneness).

5. Serve with desired fixings, such as keto tortillas, lettuce, sour cream, avocado slices, shredded Cheddar cheese, and coriander.

## Herb-Roasted Beef Tips with Onions

**Prep time: 5 minutes | Cook time: 10 minutes | Serves 4**

| 450 g rib eye steak, cubed | 1 teaspoon salt |
| 2 garlic cloves, minced | ½ teaspoon black pepper |
| 2 tablespoons olive oil | 1 brown onion, thinly sliced |
| 1 tablespoon fresh oregano | |

Cook:

1. Set the air fryer to 190ºC.

2. In a medium bowl, combine the steak, garlic, olive oil, oregano, salt, pepper, and onion. Mix until all of the beef and

onion are well coated.
3. Put the seasoned steak mixture into the air fryer drawer. Roast for 5 minutes. Stir and roast for 5 minutes more.
4. Let rest for 5 minutes before serving with some favourite sides.

## Goat Cheese-Stuffed Bavette Steak

**Prep time: 10 minutes | Cook time: 14 minutes | Serves 6**

| | |
|---|---|
| 450 g bavette or skirt steak | ¼ teaspoon freshly ground black pepper |
| 1 tablespoon avocado oil | 60 g goat cheese, crumbled |
| ½ teaspoon sea salt | 235 g baby spinach, chopped |
| ½ teaspoon garlic powder | |

**Cook:**
1. Place the steak in a large zip-top bag or between two pieces of plastic wrap. Using a meat mallet or heavy-bottomed skillet, pound the steak to an even ¼-inch thickness.
2. Brush both sides of the steak with the avocado oil.
3. Mix the salt, garlic powder, and pepper in a small dish. Sprinkle this mixture over both sides of the steak.
4. Sprinkle the goat cheese over top, and top that with the spinach.
5. Starting at one of the long sides, roll the steak up tightly. Tie the rolled steak with kitchen string at 3-inch intervals.
6. Set the air fryer to 200°C. Place the steak roll-up in the air fryer drawer. Air fry for 7 minutes. Flip the steak and cook for an additional 7 minutes, until an instant-read thermometer reads 49°C for medium-rare (adjust the cooking time for your desired doneness).

## Garlic Butter Steak Bites

**Prep time: 5 minutes | Cook time: 16 minutes | Serves 3**

| | |
|---|---|
| Oil, for spraying | sauce |
| 450 g boneless steak, cut into 1-inch pieces | ½ teaspoon granulated garlic |
| 2 tablespoons olive oil | ½ teaspoon salt |
| 1 teaspoon Worcestershire | ¼ teaspoon freshly ground black pepper |

**Cook:**
1. Set the air fryer to 200°C. Line the air fryer drawer with parchment and spray lightly with oil.
2. In a medium bowl, combine the steak, olive oil, Worcestershire sauce, garlic, salt, and black pepper and toss until evenly coated.
3. Place the steak in a single layer in the prepared drawer. You may have to work in batches, depending on the size of your air fryer.
4. Cook for 10 to 16 minutes, flipping every 3 to 4 minutes. The total cooking time will depend on the thickness of the meat and your preferred doneness. If you want it well done, it may take up to 5 additional minutes.

## Mushroom in Bacon-Wrapped Filets Mignons

**Prep time: 10 minutes | Cook time: 13 minutes per batch | Serves 8**

| | |
|---|---|
| 30 g dried porcini mushrooms | ½ teaspoon ground white pepper |
| ½ teaspoon granulated white sugar | 8 (110 g) filets mignons or beef fillet steaks |
| ½ teaspoon salt | 8 thin-cut bacon strips |

**Cook:**
1. Set the air fryer to 200°C.
2. Put the mushrooms, sugar, salt, and white pepper in a spice grinder and grind to combine.
3. On a clean work surface, rub the filets mignons with the mushroom mixture, then wrap each filet with a bacon strip. Secure with toothpicks if necessary.
4. Arrange the bacon-wrapped filets mignons in the set air fryer drawer, seam side down. Work in batches to avoid overcrowding.
5. Air fry for 13 minutes or until medium rare. Flip the filets halfway through.
6. Serve immediately.

## Sausage and Pork Meatballs

**Prep time: 15 minutes | Cook time: 8 to 12 minutes | Serves 8**

| | |
|---|---|
| 1 large egg | 1 tablespoon tomato paste |
| 1 teaspoon gelatin | 1 teaspoon minced garlic |
| 450 g pork mince | 1 teaspoon dried oregano |
| 230 g Italian-seasoned sausage, casings removed, crumbled | ¼ teaspoon red pepper flakes |
| | Sea salt and freshly ground black pepper, to taste |
| 80 g Parmesan cheese | Keto-friendly marinara sauce, for serving |
| 60 g finely diced onion | |

**Cook:**
1. Beat the egg in a small bowl and sprinkle with the gelatin. Allow to sit for 5 minutes.
2. In a large bowl, combine the pork mince, sausage, Parmesan,

onion, tomato paste, garlic, oregano, and red pepper flakes. Season with salt and black pepper.
3. Stir the gelatin mixture, then add it to the other ingredients and, using clean hands, mix to ensure that everything is well combined. form into 1½-inch round meatballs.
4. Set the air fryer to 200°C. Place the meatballs in the air fryer drawer in a single layer, cooking in batches as needed. Air fry for 5 minutes. Flip and cook for 3 to 7 minutes more, or until an instant-read thermometer reads 72°C.

## Mustard Herb Pork Tenderloin

### Prep time: 5 minutes | Cook time: 20 minutes | Serves 6

| 60 ml mayonnaise | 1 (450 g) pork tenderloin |
| 2 tablespoons Dijon mustard | ½ teaspoon salt |
| ½ teaspoon dried thyme | ¼ teaspoon ground black pepper |
| ¼ teaspoon dried rosemary | |

Cook:
1. In a small bowl, mix mayonnaise, mustard, thyme, and rosemary. Brush tenderloin with mixture on all sides, then sprinkle with salt and pepper on all sides.
2. Place tenderloin into ungreased air fryer drawer. Adjust the temperature to 200°C and air fry for 20 minutes, turning tenderloin halfway through cooking. Tenderloin will be golden and have an internal temperature of at least 64°C when done. Serve warm.

## Zesty London Broil

### Prep time: 30 minutes | Cook time: 20 to 28 minutes | Serves 4 to 6

| 160 ml ketchup | 2 tablespoons minced onion |
| 60 ml honey | ½ teaspoon paprika |
| 60 ml olive oil | 1 teaspoon salt |
| 2 tablespoons apple cider vinegar | 1 teaspoon freshly ground black pepper |
| 2 tablespoons Worcestershire sauce | 900 g bavette or skirt steak (about 1-inch thick) |

Cook:
1. Combine the ketchup, honey, olive oil, apple cider vinegar, Worcestershire sauce, minced onion, paprika, salt and pepper in a small bowl and whisk together.
2. Generously pierce both sides of the meat with a fork or meat tenderizer and place it in a shallow dish. Pour the marinade mixture over the steak, making sure all sides of the meat get coated with the marinade. Cover and refrigerate overnight.
3. Set the air fryer to 200°C.
4. Transfer the steak to the air fryer drawer and air fry for 20 to 28 minutes, depending on how rare or well done you like your steak. Flip the steak over halfway through the cooking time.
5. Remove the steak from the air fryer and let it rest for five minutes on a cutting board. To serve, thinly slice the meat against the grain and transfer to a serving platter.

## Mexican-Style Shredded Beef

### Prep time: 5 minutes | Cook time: 35 minutes | Serves 6

| 1 (900 g) beef braising steak, cut into 2-inch cubes | pepper |
| 1 teaspoon salt | 120 ml no-sugar-added chipotle sauce |
| ½ teaspoon ground black | |

Cook:
1. In a large bowl, sprinkle beef cubes with salt and pepper and toss to coat. Place beef into ungreased air fryer drawer. Adjust the temperature to 200°C and air fry for 30 minutes, shaking the drawer halfway through cooking. Beef will be done when internal temperature is at least 72°C.
2. Place cooked beef into a large bowl and shred with two forks. Pour in chipotle sauce and toss to coat. 3. Return beef to air fryer drawer for an additional 5 minutes at 200°C to crisp with sauce. Serve warm.

## Tuscan Air Fried Veal Loin

### Prep time: 1 hour 10 minutes | Cook time: 12 minutes | Makes 3 veal chops

| 1½ teaspoons crushed fennel seeds | 1½ teaspoons salt |
| 1 tablespoon minced fresh rosemary leaves | ½ teaspoon red pepper flakes |
| 1 tablespoon minced garlic | 2 tablespoons olive oil |
| 1½ teaspoons lemon zest | 3 (280 g) bone-in veal loin, about ½ inch thick |

Cook:
1. Combine all the ingredients, except for the veal loin, in a large bowl. Stir to mix well.
2. Dunk the loin in the mixture and press to submerge. Wrap the bowl in plastic and refrigerate for at least an hour to marinate.
3. Set the air fryer to 200°C.
4. Arrange the veal loin in the set air fryer and air fry for 12 minutes for medium-rare, or until it reaches your desired doneness.
5. Serve immediately.

# Chapter 6   Fish and Seafood

## Bacon-Wrapped Scallops

**Prep time: 5 minutes | Cook time: 10 minutes | Serves 4**

| | |
|---|---|
| 8 sea scallops, 30 g each, cleaned and patted dry | ¼ teaspoon salt |
| 8 slices bacon | ¼ teaspoon ground black pepper |

Cook:

1. Wrap each scallop in 1 slice bacon and secure with a toothpick. Sprinkle with salt and pepper.
2. Place scallops into ungreased air fryer drawer. Adjust the temperature to 180ºC and air fry for 10 minutes. Scallops will be opaque and firm, and have an internal temperature of 56ºC when done.
3. Serve warm.

## Sole and Asparagus Bundles

**Prep time: 10 minutes | Cook time: 14 minutes | Serves 2**

| | |
|---|---|
| 230 g asparagus, trimmed | butter, softened |
| 1 teaspoon extra-virgin olive oil, divided | 1 small shallot, minced |
| Salt and pepper, to taste | 1 tablespoon chopped fresh tarragon |
| 4 (85 g) skinless sole fillets, ⅛ to ¼ inch thick | ¼ teaspoon lemon zest plus ½ teaspoon juice |
| 4 tablespoons unsalted | Vegetable oil spray |

Cook:

1. Set the air fryer to 150ºC.
2. Toss asparagus with ½ teaspoon oil, pinch salt, and pinch pepper in a bowl. Cover and microwave until bright green and just tender, about 3 minutes, tossing halfway through microwaving. Uncover and set aside to cool slightly.
3. Make foil sling for air fryer drawer by folding 1 long sheet of aluminum foil so it is 4 inches wide. Lay sheet of foil widthwise across drawer, pressing foil into and up sides of drawer. Fold excess foil as needed so that edges of foil are flush with top of drawer. Lightly spray foil and drawer with vegetable oil spray.
4. Pat sole dry with paper towels and season with salt and pepper. Arrange fillets skinned side up on cutting board, with thicker ends closest to you. Arrange asparagus evenly across base of each fillet, then tightly roll fillets away from you around asparagus to form tidy bundles.
5. Rub bundles evenly with remaining ½ teaspoon oil and arrange seam side down on sling in prepared drawer. Bake until asparagus is tender and sole flakes apart when gently prodded with a paring knife, 14 to 18 minutes, using a sling to rotate bundles halfway through cooking.
6. Combine butter, shallot, tarragon, and lemon zest and juice in a bowl. Using sling, carefully remove sole bundles from air fryer and transfer to individual plates. Top evenly with butter mixture and serve.

## Golden Prawns

**Prep time: 20 minutes | Cook time: 7 minutes | Serves 4**

| | |
|---|---|
| 2 egg whites | 1 teaspoon garlic powder |
| 30 g coconut flour | ½ teaspoon dried rosemary |
| 120 g Parmigiano-Reggiano, grated | ½ teaspoon sea salt |
| ½ teaspoon celery seeds | ½ teaspoon ground black pepper |
| ½ teaspoon porcini powder | 680 g prawns, peeled and deveined |
| ½ teaspoon onion powder | |

Cook:

1. Whisk the egg with coconut flour and Parmigiano-Reggiano. Add in seasonings and mix to combine well.
2. Dip your prawns in the batter. Roll until they are covered on all sides.
3. Cook in the set air fryer at 200ºC for 5 to 7 minutes or until golden brown. Work in batches.
4. Serve with lemon wedges if desired.

## Paprika Crab Burgers

**Prep time: 30 minutes | Cook time: 14 minutes | Serves 3**

| | |
|---|---|
| 2 eggs, beaten | 280 g crab meat |
| 1 shallot, chopped | 1 teaspoon smoked paprika |
| 2 garlic cloves, crushed | ½ teaspoon ground black pepper |
| 1 tablespoon olive oil | Sea salt, to taste |
| 1 teaspoon yellow mustard | 70 g Parmesan cheese |
| 1 teaspoon fresh coriander, chopped | |

Cook:

1. In a mixing bowl, thoroughly combine the eggs, shallot, garlic, olive oil, mustard, coriander, crab meat, paprika, black pepper, and salt. Mix until well combined.
2. Shape the mixture into 6 patties. Roll the crab patties over grated Parmesan cheese, coating well on all sides. Place in your refrigerator for 2 hours.
3. Spritz the crab patties with cooking oil on both sides. Cook in the set air fryer at 180ºC for 14 minutes. Serve on dinner rolls if desired. Bon appétit!

## Steamed Tuna with Lemongrass

**Prep time: 10 minutes | Cook time: 10 minutes | Serves 4**

| | |
|---|---|
| 4 small tuna steaks | fresh ginger |
| 2 tablespoons low-sodium soy sauce | ⅛ teaspoon freshly ground black pepper |
| 2 teaspoons sesame oil | 1 stalk lemongrass, bent in half |
| 2 teaspoons rice wine vinegar | 3 tablespoons freshly squeezed lemon juice |
| 1 teaspoon grated peeled | |

Cook:

1. Place the tuna steaks on a plate.
2. In a small bowl, whisk the soy sauce, sesame oil, vinegar, and ginger until combined. Pour this mixture over the tuna and gently rub it into both sides. Sprinkle the fish with the pepper. Let marinate for 10 minutes.
3. Insert the crisper plate into the drawer and the drawer into the unit. Set the unit to 200°C.
4. Once the unit is set, place the lemongrass into the drawer and top it with the tuna steaks. Drizzle the tuna with the lemon juice and 1 tablespoon of water.
5. Cook for 10 minutes.
6. When the cooking is complete, a food thermometer inserted into the tuna should register at least 64°C. Discard the lemongrass and serve the tuna.

## Fish Croquettes with Lemon-Dill Aioli

**Prep time: 15 minutes | Cook time: 10 minutes | Serves 4**

| | |
|---|---|
| Croquettes: | 1 teaspoon fresh lemon juice |
| 3 large eggs, divided | 1 teaspoon kosher or coarse sea salt |
| 340 g raw cod fillet, flaked apart with two forks | ½ teaspoon dried thyme |
| 60 ml skimmed milk | ¼ teaspoon freshly ground black pepper |
| 190 g boxed instant mashed potatoes | Cooking spray |
| 2 teaspoons olive oil | Lemon-Dill Aioli: |
| 8 g chopped fresh dill | 5 tablespoons mayonnaise |
| 1 shallot, minced | Juice of ½ lemon |
| 1 large garlic clove, minced | 1 tablespoon chopped fresh dill |
| 60 g breadcrumbs plus 2 tablespoons, divided | |

Cook:

1. For the croquettes: In a medium bowl, lightly beat 2 of the eggs. Add the fish, milk, instant mashed potatoes, olive oil, dill, shallot, and garlic, 2 tablespoons of the bread crumbs, lemon juice, salt, thyme, and pepper. Mix to thoroughly combine. Place in the refrigerator for 30 minutes.
2. For the lemon-dill aioli: In a small bowl, combine the mayonnaise, lemon juice, and dill. Set aside.
3. Measure out about 3½ tablespoons of the fish mixture and gently roll in your hands to form a log about 3 inches long. Repeat to make a total of 12 logs.
4. Beat the remaining egg in a small bowl. Place the remaining ¾ cup bread crumbs in a separate bowl. Dip the croquettes in the egg, then coat in the bread crumbs, gently pressing to adhere. Place on a work surface and spray both sides with cooking spray.
5. Set the air fryer to 180°C.
6. Working in batches, arrange a single layer of the croquettes in the air fryer drawer. Air fry for about 10 minutes, flipping halfway, until golden.
7. Serve with the aioli for dipping.

## Tuna Cakes

**Prep time: 10 minutes | Cook time: 10 minutes | Serves 4**

| | |
|---|---|
| 4 (85 g) tuna fillets, drained | chopped white onion |
| 1 large egg, whisked | ½ teaspoon Old Bay seasoning |
| 2 tablespoons peeled and | |

Cook:

1. In a large bowl, mix all ingredients together and form into four patties.
2. Place patties into ungreased air fryer drawer. Adjust the temperature to 200°C and air fry for 10 minutes. Patties will be browned and crispy when done. Let cool 5 minutes before serving.

## Prawns with Smoky Tomato Dressing

**Prep time: 5 minutes | Cook time: 8 minutes | Serves 2**

| | |
|---|---|
| 3 tablespoons mayonnaise | sea salt |
| 1 tablespoon ketchup | 455 g large raw prawns (21 to 25 count), peeled (tails left on) and deveined |
| 1 tablespoon minced garlic | |
| 1 teaspoon Sriracha | Vegetable oil spray |
| ½ teaspoon smoked paprika | |
| ½ teaspoon kosher or coarse | 50 g chopped spring onions |

Cook:

1. In a large bowl, combine the mayonnaise, ketchup, garlic, Sriracha, paprika, and salt. Add the prawns and toss to coat with the sauce.
2. Spray the air fryer drawer with vegetable oil spray. Place the prawns in the drawer. Set the air fryer to 180°C for 8 minutes, tossing and spraying the prawns with vegetable oil spray halfway through the cooking time.
3. Sprinkle with the chopped spring onions before serving.

## Snapper Scampi

**Prep time: 5 minutes | Cook time: 8 to 10 minutes | Serves 4**

| 4 skinless snapper or arctic char fillets, 170 g each | Pinch salt |
| 1 tablespoon olive oil | Freshly ground black pepper, to taste |
| 3 tablespoons lemon juice, divided | 2 tablespoons butter |
| ½ teaspoon dried basil | 2 cloves garlic, minced |

Cook:
1. Rub the fish fillets with olive oil and 1 tablespoon of the lemon juice. Sprinkle with the basil, salt, and pepper, and place in the air fryer drawer.
2. Air fry the fish at 190°C for 7 to 8 minutes or until the fish just flakes when tested with a fork. Remove the fish from the drawer and put on a serving plate. Cover to keep warm.
3. In a baking dish, combine the butter, remaining 2 tablespoons lemon juice, and garlic. Bake in the air fryer for 1 to 2 minutes or until the garlic is sizzling. Pour this mixture over the fish and serve.

## Cod with Avocado

**Prep time: 30 minutes | Cook time: 10 minutes | Serves 2**

| 90 g shredded cabbage | 1 teaspoon chilli powder |
| 60 ml full-fat sour cream | 1 teaspoon cumin |
| 2 tablespoons full-fat mayonnaise | ½ teaspoon paprika |
| 20 g chopped pickled jalapeños | ¼ teaspoon garlic powder |
| 2 (85 g) cod fillets | 1 medium avocado, peeled, pitted, and sliced |
| | ½ medium lime |

Cook:
1. In a large bowl, place cabbage, sour cream, mayonnaise, and jalapeños. Mix until fully coated. Let sit for 20 minutes in the refrigerator.
2. Sprinkle cod fillets with chilli powder, cumin, paprika, and garlic powder. Place each fillet into the air fryer drawer.
3. Adjust the temperature to 190°C and set the timer for 10 minutes.
4. Flip the fillets halfway through the cooking time. When fully cooked, fish should have an internal temperature of at least 64°C.
5. To serve, divide slaw mixture into two serving bowls, break cod fillets into pieces and spread over the bowls, and top with avocado. Squeeze lime juice over each bowl. Serve immediately.

## Air Fryer Fish Fry

**Prep time: 5 minutes | Cook time: 15 minutes | Serves 4**

| 470 ml low-fat buttermilk | 35 g plain yellow cornmeal |
| ½ teaspoon garlic powder | 25 g chickpea flour |
| ½ teaspoon onion powder | ¼ teaspoon cayenne pepper |
| 4 (110 g) sole fillets | Freshly ground black pepper |

Cook:
1. In a large bowl, combine the buttermilk, garlic powder, and onion powder.
2. Add the sole, turning until well coated, and set aside to marinate for 20 minutes.
3. In a shallow bowl, stir the cornmeal, chickpea flour, cayenne, and pepper together.
4. Dredge the fillets in the meal mixture, turning until well coated. Place in the drawer of an air fryer.
5. Set the air fryer to 190°C, close, and cook for 12 minutes.

## Fried Catfish with Dijon Sauce

**Prep time: 20 minutes | Cook time: 7 minutes | Serves 4**

| 4 tablespoons butter, melted | 4 catfish fillets, 110g each |
| 2 teaspoons Worcestershire sauce, divided | Cooking spray |
| | 120 ml sour cream |
| 1 teaspoon lemon pepper | 1 tablespoon Dijon mustard |
| 60 g panko bread crumbs | |

Cook:
1. In a shallow bowl, stir together the melted butter, 1 teaspoon of Worcestershire sauce, and the lemon pepper. Place the bread crumbs in another shallow bowl.
2. One at a time, dip both sides of the fillets in the butter mixture, then the bread crumbs, coating thoroughly.
3. Set the air fryer to 150°C. Line the air fryer drawer with baking paper.

4. Place the coated fish on the baking paper and spritz with oil.
5. Bake for 4 minutes. Flip the fish, spritz it with oil, and bake for 3 to 6 minutes more, depending on the thickness of the fillets, until the fish flakes easily with a fork.
6. In a small bowl, stir together the sour cream, Dijon, and remaining 1 teaspoon of Worcestershire sauce. This sauce can be made 1 day in advance and refrigerated before serving. Serve with the fried fish.

## Scallops and Spinach with Cream Sauce

**Prep time: 5 minutes | Cook time: 10 minutes | Serves 2**

| | |
|---|---|
| Vegetable oil spray | 180 ml heavy cream |
| 280 g frozen spinach, thawed and drained | 1 tablespoon tomato paste |
| 8 jumbo sea scallops | 1 tablespoon chopped fresh basil |
| Kosher or coarse sea salt, and black pepper, to taste | 1 teaspoon minced garlic |

Cook:
1. Spray a baking dish with vegetable oil spray. Spread the thawed spinach in an even layer in the bottom of the pan.
2. Spray both sides of the scallops with vegetable oil spray. Season lightly with salt and pepper. Arrange the scallops on top of the spinach.
3. In a small bowl, whisk together the cream, tomato paste, basil, garlic, ½ teaspoon salt, and ½ teaspoon pepper. Pour the sauce over the scallops and spinach.
4. Place the pan in the air fryer drawer. Set the air fryer to 180ºC for 10 minutes. Use a meat thermometer to ensure the scallops have an internal temperature of 56ºC.

## Crab and Bell Pepper Cakes

**Prep time: 5 minutes | Cook time: 10 minutes | Serves 4**

| | |
|---|---|
| 230 g jumbo lump crabmeat | 1 egg |
| 1 tablespoon Old Bay seasoning | 60 g mayonnaise |
| 20 g bread crumbs | Juice of ½ lemon |
| 40 g diced red bell pepper | 1 teaspoon plain flour |
| 40 g diced green bell pepper | Cooking oil spray |

Cook:
1. Sort through the crabmeat, picking out any bits of shell or cartilage.
2. In a large bowl, stir together the Old Bay seasoning, bread crumbs, red and green bell peppers, egg, mayonnaise, and lemon juice. Gently stir in the crabmeat.
3. Insert the crisper plate into the drawer and the drawer into the unit. Set the unit to 190ºC.
4. Form the mixture into 4 patties. Sprinkle ¼ teaspoon of flour on top of each patty.
5. Once the unit is set, spray the crisper plate with cooking oil. Place the crab cakes into the drawer and spray them with cooking oil.
6. Cook for 10 minutes.
7. When the cooking is complete, the crab cakes will be golden brown and firm.

## Chilli Tilapia

**Prep time: 5 minutes | Cook time: 20 minutes | Serves 4**

| | |
|---|---|
| 4 tilapia fillets, boneless | 1 tablespoon avocado oil |
| 1 teaspoon chilli flakes | 1 teaspoon mustard |
| 1 teaspoon dried oregano | |

Cook:
1. Rub the tilapia fillets with chilli flakes, dried oregano, avocado oil, and mustard and put in the air fryer.
2. Cook it for 10 minutes per side at 180ºC.

## Orange-Mustard Glazed Salmon

**Prep time: 10 minutes | Cook time: 10 minutes | Serves 2**

| | |
|---|---|
| 1 tablespoon orange marmalade | mustard |
| ¼ teaspoon grated orange zest plus 1 tablespoon juice | 2 (230 g) skin-on salmon fillets, 1½ inches thick |
| 2 teaspoons whole-grain | Salt and pepper, to taste |
| | Vegetable oil spray |

Cook:
1. Set the air fryer to 200ºC.
2. Make foil sling for air fryer drawer by folding 1 long sheet of aluminum foil so it is 4 inches wide. Lay sheet of foil widthwise across drawer, pressing foil into and up sides of drawer. Fold excess foil as needed so that edges of foil are flush with top of drawer. Lightly spray foil and drawer with vegetable oil spray.
3. Combine marmalade, orange zest and juice, and mustard in bowl. Pat salmon dry with paper towels and season with salt and pepper. Brush tops and sides of fillets evenly with glaze. Arrange fillets skin side down on sling in prepared drawer, spaced evenly apart. Air fry salmon until center is still

translucent when checked with the tip of a paring knife and registers 52°C (for medium-rare), 10 to 14 minutes, using sling to rotate fillets halfway through cooking.
4. Using the sling, carefully remove salmon from air fryer. Slide fish spatula along underside of fillets and transfer to individual serving plates, leaving skin behind.
5. Serve.

## Almond Pesto Salmon

**Prep time: 5 minutes | Cook time: 12 minutes | Serves 2**

| | |
|---|---|
| 60 g pesto | fillets (about 110 g each) |
| 20 g sliced almonds, roughly chopped | 2 tablespoons unsalted butter, melted |
| 2 (1½-inch-thick) salmon | |

Cook:

1. In a small bowl, mix pesto and almonds. Set aside.
2. Place fillets into a round baking dish.
3. Brush each fillet with butter and place half of the pesto mixture on the top of each fillet. Place dish into the air fryer drawer.
4. Adjust the temperature to 200°C and set the timer for 12 minutes.
5. Salmon will easily flake when fully cooked and reach an internal temperature of at least 64°C.
6. Serve warm.

## Parmesan-Crusted Hake with Garlic Sauce

**Prep time: 5 minutes | Cook time: 10 minutes | Serves 3**

**Fish:**

| | |
|---|---|
| 6 tablespoons mayonnaise | Salt, to taste |
| 1 tablespoon fresh lime juice | ¼ teaspoon ground black pepper, or more to taste |
| 1 teaspoon Dijon mustard | 3 hake fillets, patted dry |
| 150 g grated Parmesan cheese | Nonstick cooking spray |

**Garlic Sauce:**

| | |
|---|---|
| 60 ml plain Greek yogurt | ½ teaspoon minced tarragon leaves |
| 2 tablespoons olive oil | |
| 2 cloves garlic, minced | |

Cook:

1. Set the air fryer to 200°C.
2. Mix the mayo, lime juice, and mustard in a shallow bowl and whisk to combine. In another shallow bowl, stir together the grated Parmesan cheese, salt, and pepper.
3. Dredge each fillet in the mayo mixture, then roll them in the cheese mixture until they are evenly coated on both sides.
4. Spray the air fryer drawer with nonstick cooking spray. Arrange the fillets in the drawer and air fry for 10 minutes, or until the fish flakes easily with a fork. Flip the fillets halfway through the cooking time.
5. Meanwhile, in a small bowl, whisk all the ingredients for the sauce until well incorporated.
6. Serve the fish warm alongside the sauce.

## Blackened Red Snapper

**Prep time: 13 minutes | Cook time: 8 to 10 minutes | Serves 4**

| | |
|---|---|
| 1½ teaspoons black pepper | 4 red snapper fillet portions, skin on, 110 g each |
| ¼ teaspoon thyme | 4 thin slices lemon |
| ¼ teaspoon garlic powder | Cooking spray |
| ⅛ teaspoon cayenne pepper | |
| 1 teaspoon olive oil | |

Cook:

1. Mix the spices and oil together to make a paste. Rub into both sides of the fish.
2. Spray the air fryer drawer with nonstick cooking spray and lay snapper steaks in drawer, skin-side down.
3. Place a lemon slice on each piece of fish.
4. Roast at 200°C for 8 to 10 minutes. The fish will not flake when done, but it should be white through the center.

## Bang Bang Prawns

**Prep time: 15 minutes | Cook time: 14 minutes | Serves 4**

**Sauce:**

| | |
|---|---|
| 115 g mayonnaise | 1 teaspoon minced fresh ginger |
| 60 ml sweet chilli sauce | |
| 2 to 4 tablespoons Sriracha | |

**Prawns:**

| | |
|---|---|
| 455 g jumbo raw prawns (21 to 25 count), peeled and deveined | rice flour |
| | ½ teaspoon kosher or coarse sea salt |
| 2 tablespoons cornflour or | Vegetable oil spray |

Cook:

1. For the sauce: In a large bowl, combine the mayonnaise, chilli sauce, Sriracha, and ginger. Stir until well combined.

Remove half of the sauce to serve as a dipping sauce.

2. For the prawns: Place the prawns in a medium bowl. Sprinkle the cornflour and salt over the prawns and toss until well coated.

3. Place the prawns in the air fryer drawer in a single layer. (If they won't fit in a single layer, set a rack or trivet on top of the bottom layer of prawns and place the rest of the prawns on the rack.) Spray generously with vegetable oil spray. Set the air fryer to 180ºC for 10 minutes, turning and spraying with additional oil spray halfway through the cooking time.

4. Remove the prawns and toss in the bowl with half of the sauce. Place the prawns back in the air fryer drawer. Cook for an additional 4 to 5 minutes, or until the sauce has formed a glaze.

5. Serve the hot prawns with the reserved sauce for dipping.

## Crab Cakes

**Prep time: 10 minutes | Cook time: 10 minutes | Serves 4**

| | |
|---|---|
| 2 cans lump crab meat, 170 g each | ½ teaspoon Dijon mustard |
| ¼ cup blanched finely ground almond flour | ½ tablespoon lemon juice |
| | ½ medium green bell pepper, seeded and chopped |
| 1 large egg | 235 g chopped spring onion |
| 2 tablespoons full-fat mayonnaise | ½ teaspoon Old Bay seasoning |

Cook:

1. In a large bowl, combine all ingredients. form into four balls and flatten into patties. Place patties into the air fryer drawer.
2. Adjust the temperature to 180ºC and air fry for 10 minutes.
3. Flip patties halfway through the cooking time. Serve warm.

## Fried Catfish Fillets

**Prep time: 10 minutes | Cook time: 20 minutes | Serves 4**

| | |
|---|---|
| 1 egg | ¼ teaspoon garlic powder |
| 50 g finely ground cornmeal | ¼ teaspoon freshly ground black pepper |
| 20 g plain flour | |
| ¾ teaspoon salt | 4 140 g catfish fillets, halved crosswise |
| 1 teaspoon paprika | |
| 1 teaspoon Old Bay seasoning | Olive oil spray |

Cook:

1. In a shallow bowl, beat the egg with 2 tablespoons water.

2. On a plate, stir together the cornmeal, flour, salt, paprika, Old Bay, garlic powder, and pepper.

3. Dip the fish into the egg mixture and into the cornmeal mixture to coat. Press the cornmeal mixture into the fish and gently shake off any excess.

4. Insert the crisper plate into the drawer and the drawer into the unit to 200ºC.

5. Once the unit is set, place a baking paper liner into the drawer. Place the coated fish on the liner and spray it with olive oil.

6. Cook for 10 minutes, remove the drawer and spray the fish with olive oil. Flip the fish and spray the other side with olive oil. Reinsert the drawer to resume cooking. Check the fish after 7 minutes more. If the fish is golden and crispy and registers at least 64ºC on a food thermometer, it is ready. If not, resume cooking.

7. When the cooking is complete, serve.

## Dukkah-Crusted Halibut

**Prep time: 15 minutes | Cook time: 17 minutes | Serves 2**

**Dukkah:**

| | |
|---|---|
| 1 tablespoon coriander seeds | ¼ teaspoon kosher or coarse sea salt |
| 1 tablespoon sesame seeds | |
| 1½ teaspoons cumin seeds | ¼ teaspoon black pepper |
| 50 g roasted mixed nuts | |

**Fish:**

| | |
|---|---|
| 2 halibut fillets, 140 g each | Vegetable oil spray |
| 2 tablespoons mayonnaise | Lemon wedges, for serving |

Cook:

1. for the Dukkah: Combine the coriander, sesame seeds, and cumin in a small baking dish. Place the pan in the air fryer drawer. Set the air fryer to 200ºC for 5 minutes. Toward the end of the cooking time, you will hear the seeds popping. Transfer to a plate and let cool for 5 minutes.

2. Transfer the toasted seeds to a food processor or spice grinder and add the mixed nuts. Pulse until coarsely chopped. Add the salt and pepper and stir well.

3. For the fish: Spread each fillet with 1 tablespoon of the mayonnaise. Press a heaping tablespoon of the Dukkah into the mayonnaise on each fillet, pressing lightly to adhere.

4. Spray the air fryer drawer with vegetable oil spray. Place the fish in the drawer. Cook for 12 minutes, or until the fish flakes easily with a fork.

5. Serve the fish with lemon wedges.

## Friday Night Fish-Fry

**Prep time: 10 minutes | Cook time: 10 minutes | Serves 4**

| | |
|---|---|
| 1 large egg | 4 cod fillets, 110 g each |
| 25 g powdered Parmesan cheese | Chopped fresh oregano or parsley, for garnish (optional) |
| 1 teaspoon smoked paprika | Lemon slices, for serving (optional) |
| ¼ teaspoon celery salt | |
| ¼ teaspoon ground black pepper | |

Cook:

1. Spray the air fryer drawer with avocado oil. Set the air fryer to 200°C.
2. Crack the egg in a shallow bowl and beat it lightly with a fork. Combine the Parmesan cheese, paprika, celery salt, and pepper in a separate shallow bowl.
3. One at a time, dip the fillets into the egg, then dredge them in the Parmesan mixture. Using your hands, press the Parmesan onto the fillets to form a nice crust. As you finish, place the fish in the air fryer drawer.
4. Air fry the fish in the air fryer for 10 minutes, or until it is cooked through and flakes easily with a fork. Garnish with fresh oregano or parsley and serve with lemon slices, if desired.
5. Store leftovers in an airtight container in the refrigerator for up to 3 days. Reheat in a set 200°C air fryer for 5 minutes, or until warmed through.

## Mustard-Crusted Fish Fillets

**Prep time: 5 minutes | Cook time: 8 to 11 minutes | Serves 4**

| | |
|---|---|
| 5 teaspoons yellow mustard | ⅛ teaspoon freshly ground black pepper |
| 1 tablespoon freshly squeezed lemon juice | 1 slice whole-wheat bread, crumbled |
| 4 sole fillets, 100 g each | 2 teaspoons olive oi |
| ½ teaspoon dried thyme | |
| ½ teaspoon dried marjoram | |

Cook:

1. In a small bowl, mix the mustard and lemon juice. Spread this evenly over the fillets. Place them in the air fryer drawer.
2. In another small bowl, mix the thyme, marjoram, pepper, bread crumbs, and olive oil. Mix until combined.
3. Gently but firmly press the spice mixture onto the top of each fish fillet.
4. Bake at 160°C for 8 to 11 minutes, or until the fish reaches an internal temperature of at least 64°C on a meat thermometer and the topping is browned and crisp.
5. Serve immediately.

# Chapter 7  Snacks and Appetizers

## Carrot Chips

**Prep time: 15 minutes | Cook time: 8 to 10 minutes | Serves 4**

| | |
|---|---|
| 1 tablespoon olive oil, plus more for greasing the drawer | trimmed and thinly sliced |
| 4 to 5 medium carrots, | 1 teaspoon seasoned salt |

Cook:
1. Set the air fryer to 200ºC. Grease the air fryer drawer with the olive oil.
2. Toss the carrot slices with 1 tablespoon of olive oil and salt in a medium-sized bowl until thoroughly coated.
3. Arrange the carrot slices in the greased drawer. You may need to work in batches to avoid overcrowding.
4. Air fry for 8 to 10 minutes until the carrot slices are crisp-tender. Shake the drawer once during cooking.
5. Transfer the carrot slices to a bowl and repeat with the remaining carrots.
6. Allow to cool for 5 minutes and serve.

## Hush Puppies

**Prep time: 45 minutes | Cook time: 10 minutes | Serves 12**

| | |
|---|---|
| 144 g self-raising yellow cornmeal | 80 g canned creamed sweetcorn |
| 60 g plain flour | 216 g minced onion |
| 1 teaspoon sugar | 2 teaspoons minced jalapeño chillies pepper |
| 1 teaspoon salt | |
| 1 teaspoon freshly ground black pepper | 2 tablespoons olive oil, divided |
| 1 large egg | |

Cook:
1. Thoroughly combine the cornmeal, flour, sugar, salt, and pepper in a large bowl.
2. Whisk together the egg and sweetcorn in a small bowl. Pour the egg mixture into the bowl of cornmeal mixture and stir to combine. Stir in the minced onion and jalapeño chillies. Cover the bowl with plastic wrap and place in the refrigerator for 30 minutes.
3. Set the air fryer to 190ºC. Line the air fryer drawer with baking paper paper and lightly brush it with 1 tablespoon of olive oil.
4. Scoop out the cornmeal mixture and form into 24 balls, about 1 inch.
5. Arrange the balls in the baking paper paper-lined drawer, leaving space between each ball.
6. Air fry in batches for 5 minutes. Shake the drawer and brush the balls with the remaining 1 tablespoon of olive oil. Continue cooking for 5 minutes until golden.
7. Remove the balls (hush puppies) from the drawer and serve on a plate.

## Garlic Edamame

**Prep time: 5 minutes | Cook time: 10 minutes | Serves 4**

| | |
|---|---|
| Olive oil | ¼ teaspoon freshly ground black pepper |
| 1 (454 g) bag frozen edamame in pods | ½ teaspoon red pepper flakes (optional) |
| ½ teaspoon salt | |
| ½ teaspoon garlic salt | |

Cook:
1. Spray the air fryer drawer lightly with olive oil.
2. In a medium-sized bowl, add the frozen edamame and lightly spray with olive oil. Toss to coat.
3. In a small bowl, mix together the salt, garlic salt, black pepper, and red pepper flakes (if using). Add the mixture to the edamame and toss until evenly coated.
4. Place half the edamame in the air fryer drawer. Do not overfill the drawer.
5. Air fry at 190ºC for 5 minutes. Shake the drawer and cook until the edamame is starting to brown and get crispy, 3 to 5 more minutes.
6. Repeat with the remaining edamame and serve immediately.

## Poutine with Waffle Fries

**Prep time: 10 minutes | Cook time: 15 to 17 minutes | Serves 4**

| | |
|---|---|
| 225 g frozen waffle cut fries | 2 spring onions, sliced |
| 2 teaspoons olive oil | 90 g shredded Swiss cheese |
| 1 red pepper, chopped | 120 ml bottled chicken gravy |

Cook:
1. Set the air fryer to 190ºC. 2. Toss the waffle fries with the olive oil and place in the air fryer drawer. Air fry for 10 to 12 minutes, or until the fries are crisp and light golden, shaking the drawer halfway through the cooking time. 3. Transfer the fries to a baking dish and top with the pepper, spring onions, and cheese. Air fry for 3 minutes, or until the mixed vegetables are crisp and tender. 4. Remove the pan from the air fryer and drizzle the gravy over the fries. Air fry for 2 minutes, or until the gravy is hot. 5. Serve immediately.

## Spinach and Crab Meat Cups

**Prep time: 10 minutes | Cook time: 10 minutes | Makes 30 cups**

| | |
|---|---|
| 1 (170 g) can crab meat, drained to yield 80 g meat | ¼ teaspoon lemon juice |
| 30 g frozen spinach, thawed, drained, and chopped | ½ teaspoon Worcestershire sauce |
| 1 clove garlic, minced | 30 mini frozen filo shells, thawed |
| 84 g grated Parmesan cheese | Cooking spray |
| 3 tablespoons plain yoghurt | |

Cook:
1. Set the air fryer to 200ºC.
2. Remove any bits of shell that might remain in the crab meat.
3. Mix the crab meat, spinach, garlic, and cheese together.
4. Stir in the yoghurt, lemon juice, and Worcestershire sauce and mix well.
5. Spoon a teaspoon of filling into each filo shell.
6. Spray the air fryer drawer with cooking spray and arrange half the shells in the drawer. Air fry for 5 minutes. Repeat with the remaining shells.
7. Serve immediately.

## Prawns Egg Rolls

**Prep time: 15 minutes | Cook time: 10 minutes per batch | Serves 4**

| | |
|---|---|
| 1 tablespoon mixed vegetables oil | 60 ml hoisin sauce |
| ½ head green or savoy cabbage, finely shredded | Freshly ground black pepper, to taste |
| 90 g grated carrots | 454 g cooked prawns, diced |
| 240 ml canned bean sprouts, drained | 30 g spring onions |
| 1 tablespoon soy sauce | 8 egg roll wrappers (or use spring roll pastry) |
| ½ teaspoon sugar | mixed vegetables oil |
| 1 teaspoon sesame oil | Duck sauce |

Cook:
1. Set a large sauté pan over medium-high heat. Add the oil and cook the cabbage, carrots and bean sprouts until they start to wilt, about 3 minutes. Add the soy sauce, sugar, sesame oil, hoisin sauce and black pepper. Sauté for a few more minutes. Stir in the prawns and spring onions and cook until the mixed vegetables are just tender. Transfer the mixture to a colander in a bowl to cool. Press or squeeze out any excess water from the filling so that you don't end up with soggy egg rolls.
2. Make the egg rolls: Place the egg roll wrappers on a flat surface with one of the points facing towards you so they look like diamonds. Dividing the filling evenly between the eight wrappers, spoon the mixture onto the centre of the egg roll wrappers. Spread the filling across the centre of the wrappers from the left corner to the right corner but leave 2 inches from each corner empty. Brush the empty sides of the wrapper with a little water. Fold the bottom corner of the wrapper tightly up over the filling, trying to avoid making any air pockets. Fold the left corner in toward the centre and then the right corner toward the centre. It should now look like an envelope. Tightly roll the egg roll from the bottom to the top open corner. Press to seal the egg roll together, brushing with a little extra water if need be. Repeat this technique with all 8 egg rolls.
3. Set the air fryer to 190ºC.
4. Spray or brush all sides of the egg rolls with mixed vegetables oil. Air fry four egg rolls at a time for 10 minutes, turning them over halfway through the cooking time.
5. Serve hot with duck sauce or your favourite dipping sauce.

## Italian Rice Balls

**Prep time: 20 minutes | Cook time: 10 minutes | Makes 8 rice balls**

| | |
|---|---|
| 355 g cooked sticky rice | (small enough to stuff into olives) |
| ½ teaspoon Italian seasoning blend | 2 eggs |
| ¾ teaspoon salt, divided | 35 g Italian breadcrumbs |
| 8 black olives, pitted | 55 g panko breadcrumbs |
| 28 g mozzarella cheese cheese, cut into tiny pieces | Cooking spray |

Cook:
1. Set air fryer to 200ºC.
2. Stuff each black olive with a piece of mozzarella cheese cheese. Set aside.
3. In a bowl, combine the cooked sticky rice, Italian seasoning blend, and ½ teaspoon of salt and stir to mix well. form the rice mixture into a log with your hands and divide it into 8 equal portions. Mould each portion around a black olive and roll into a ball.
4. Transfer to the freezer to chill for 10 to 15 minutes until firm.
5. In a shallow dish, place the Italian breadcrumbs. In a separate shallow dish, whisk the eggs. In a third shallow dish, combine the panko breadcrumbs and remaining salt.
6. One by one, roll the rice balls in the Italian breadcrumbs, then dip in the whisked eggs, finally coat them with the panko breadcrumbs.
7. Arrange the rice balls in the air fryer drawer and spritz both sides with cooking spray.
8. Air fry for 10 minutes until the rice balls are golden. Flip the balls halfway through the cooking time.
9. Serve warm.

## Honey-Mustard Chicken Wings

**Prep time: 10 minutes | Cook time: 24 minutes | Serves 2**

| | |
|---|---|
| 907 g chicken wings | 60 g spicy brown mustard |
| Salt and freshly ground black pepper, to taste | Pinch ground cayenne pepper |
| 2 tablespoons butter | 2 teaspoons Worcestershire sauce |
| 60 ml honey | |

Cook:
1. Prepare the chicken wings by cutting off the wing tips and discarding (or freezing for chicken stock). Divide the chicken drumettes from the chicken wingettes by cutting through the joint. Place the chicken wing pieces in a large bowl.
2. Set the air fryer to 200°C.
3. Season the wings with salt and freshly ground black pepper and air fry the wings in two batches for 10 minutes per batch, shaking the drawer halfway through the cooking process.
4. While the wings are air frying, combine the remaining ingredients in a small saucepan over low heat.
5. When both batches are done, toss all the wings with the honey-mustard sauce and toss them all back into the drawer for another 4 minutes to heat through and finish cooking. Give the drawer a good shake part way through the cooking process to redistribute the wings. Remove the wings from the air fryer and serve.

## Dark Chocolate and Cranberry Granola Bars

**Prep time: 5 minutes | Cook time: 15 minutes | Serves 6**

| | |
|---|---|
| 135 g certified gluten-free quick oats | 3 tablespoons unsweetened shredded coconut |
| 2 tablespoons sugar-free dark chocolate chunks | 120 ml raw honey |
| 2 tablespoons unsweetened dried cranberries | 1 teaspoon cinnamon powder |
| | ⅛ teaspoon salt |
| | 2 tablespoons olive oil |

Cook:
1. Set the air fryer to 180°C. Line an 8-by-8-inch baking dish with baking paper paper that comes up the side so you can lift it out after cooking.
2. In a large bowl, mix together all of the ingredients until well combined.
3. Press the oat mixture into the pan in an even layer.
4. Place the pan into the air fryer drawer and bake for 15 minutes.
5. Remove the pan from the air fryer and lift the granola cake out of the pan using the edges of the baking paper paper.
6. Allow to cool for 5 minutes before slicing into 6 equal bars.
7. Serve immediately or wrap in plastic wrap and store at room temperature for up to 1 week.

## Veggie Salmon Nachos

**Prep time: 10 minutes | Cook time: 9 to 12 minutes | Serves 6**

| | |
|---|---|
| 57 g baked no-salt sweetcorn tortilla chips | 50 g grated carrot |
| 1 (142 g) baked salmon fillet, flaked | 1 jalapeño chillies pepper, minced |
| 100 g canned low-salt black beans, rinsed and drained | 30 g shredded low-salt low-fat Swiss cheese |
| 1 red pepper, chopped | 1 tomato, chopped |

Cook:
1. Set the air fryer to 180°C.
2. In a baking dish, layer the tortilla chips. Top with the salmon, black beans, red pepper, carrot, jalapeño chillies, and Swiss cheese.
3. Bake in the air fryer for 9 to 12 minutes, or until the cheese is melted and starts to brown.
4. Top with the tomato and serve.

## Crunchy Basil White Beans

**Prep time: 2 minutes | Cook time: 19 minutes | Serves 2**

| | |
|---|---|
| 1 (425 g) can cooked white beans | ¼ teaspoon garlic powder |
| 2 tablespoons olive oil | ¼ teaspoon salt, divided |
| 1 teaspoon fresh sage, chopped | 1 teaspoon chopped fresh basil |

Cook:
1. Set the air fryer to 190°C.
2. In a medium-sized bowl, mix together the beans, olive oil, sage, garlic, ⅛ teaspoon salt, and basil.
3. Pour the white beans into the air fryer and spread them out in a single layer.
4. Bake for 10 minutes. Stir and continue cooking for an additional 5 to 9 minutes, or until they reach your preferred level of crispiness.
5. Toss with the remaining ⅛ teaspoon salt before serving.

## Lemon-Pepper Chicken Chicken Drumsticks

**Prep time: 30 minutes | Cook time: 30 minutes | Serves 2**

| | |
|---|---|
| 2 teaspoons freshly ground coarse black pepper | 4 chicken drumsticks (113 g each) |
| 1 teaspoon baking powder | Rock salt, to taste |
| ½ teaspoon garlic powder | 1 lemon |

Cook:

1. In a small bowl, stir together the pepper, baking powder, and garlic powder. Place the drumsticks on a plate and sprinkle evenly with the baking powder mixture, turning the drumsticks so they're well coated. Let the drumsticks stand in the refrigerator for at least 1 hour or up to overnight.
2. Sprinkle the drumsticks with salt, then transfer them to the air fryer, standing them bone-side up and leaning against the wall of the air fryer drawer. Air fry at 190ºC until fully cooked and crisp on the outside, about 30 minutes.
3. Transfer the drumsticks to a serving platter and finely grate the lemon zest over them while they're hot. Cut the lemon into wedges and serve with the warm drumsticks.

## String Bean Fries

**Prep time: 15 minutes | Cook time: 5 to 6 minutes | Serves 4**

| | |
|---|---|
| 227 g fresh French beans | ¼ teaspoon ground black pepper |
| 2 eggs | |
| 4 teaspoons water | ¼ teaspoon mustard powder (optional) |
| 60 g plain flour | |
| 50 g breadcrumbs | Oil for misting or cooking spray |
| ¼ teaspoon salt | |

Cook:

1. Set the air fryer to 180ºC.
2. Trim stem ends from French beans, wash, and pat dry.
3. In a shallow dish, beat eggs and water together until well blended.
4. Place flour in a second shallow dish.
5. In a third shallow dish, stir together the breadcrumbs, salt, pepper, and mustard powder if using.
6. Dip each bean in egg mixture, flour, egg mixture again, then breadcrumbs.
7. When you finish coating all the French beans, open air fryer and place them in drawer.
8. Cook for 3 minutes.
9. Stop and mist French beans with oil or cooking spray.
10. Cook for 2 to 3 more minutes or until French beans are crispy and nicely browned.

## Sausage Balls with Cheese

**Prep time: 10 minutes | Cook time: 10 to 11 minutes | Serves 8**

| | |
|---|---|
| 340 g mild sausage meat | 85 g soft white cheese, at room temperature |
| 177 g baking mix | |
| 120 g shredded mild Cheddar cheese | 1 to 2 tablespoons olive oil |

Cook:

1. Set the air fryer to 160ºC. Line the air fryer drawer with baking paper paper.
2. Mix together the ground sausage, baking mix, Cheddar cheese, and soft white cheese in a large bowl and stir to incorporate.
3. Divide the sausage mixture into 16 equal portions and roll them into 1-inch balls with your hands.
4. Arrange the sausage balls on the baking paper, leaving space between each ball. You may need to work in batches to avoid overcrowding.
5. Brush the sausage balls with the olive oil. Bake for 10 to 11 minutes, shaking the drawer halfway through, or until the balls are firm and lightly browned on both sides.
6. Remove from the drawer to a plate and repeat with the remaining balls.
7. Serve warm.

## Roasted Grape Dip

**Prep time: 10 minutes | Cook time: 8 to 12 minutes | Serves 6**

| | |
|---|---|
| 475 g seedless red grapes, rinsed and patted dry | yoghurt |
| | 2 tablespoons semi-skimmed milk |
| 1 tablespoon apple cider vinegar | |
| 1 tablespoon honey | 2 tablespoons minced fresh basil |
| 240 ml low-fat Greek | |

Cook:

1. In the air fryer drawer, sprinkle the grapes with the cider vinegar and drizzle with the honey. Toss to coat. Roast the grapes at 190ºC for 8 to 12 minutes, or until shrivelled but still soft. Remove from the air fryer.
2. In a medium-sized bowl, stir together the yoghurt and milk.
3. Gently blend in the grapes and basil. Serve immediately or cover and chill for 1 to 2 hours.

## Red Pepper Tapenade

**Prep time: 5 minutes | Cook time: 5 minutes | Serves 4**

| | |
|---|---|
| 1 large red pepper | and roughly chopped |
| 2 tablespoons plus 1 teaspoon olive oil, divided | 1 garlic clove, minced |
| | ½ teaspoon dried oregano |
| 120 g Kalamata olives, pitted | 1 tablespoon lemon juice |

Cook:
1. Set the air fryer to 190ºC.
2. Brush the outside of a whole red pepper with 1 teaspoon olive oil and place it inside the air fryer drawer. Roast for 5 minutes.
3. Meanwhile, in a medium-sized bowl combine the remaining 2 tablespoons of olive oil with the olives, garlic, oregano, and lemon juice.
4. Remove the red pepper from the air fryer, then gently slice off the stem and remove the seeds. Roughly chop the roasted pepper into small pieces.
5. Add the red pepper to the olive mixture and stir all together until combined.
6. Serve with pitta chips, crackers, or crusty bread.

## Grilled Ham and Cheese on Raisin Bread

**Prep time: 5 minutes | Cook time: 10 minutes | Serves 1**

| | |
|---|---|
| 2 slices raisin bread or fruit loaf | 3 slices thinly sliced honey roast ham (about 85 g) |
| 2 tablespoons butter, softened | 4 slices Muenster cheese (about 85 g) |
| 2 teaspoons honey mustard | 2 cocktail sticks |

Cook:
1. Set the air fryer to 190ºC.
2. Spread the softened butter on one side of both slices of bread and place the bread, buttered side down on the counter. Spread the honey mustard on the other side of each slice of bread. Layer 2 slices of cheese, the ham and the remaining 2 slices of cheese on one slice of bread and top with the other slice of bread. Remember to leave the buttered side of the bread on the outside.
3. Transfer the sandwich to the air fryer drawer and secure the sandwich with cocktail sticks.
4. Air fry for 5 minutes. Flip the sandwich over, remove the cocktail sticks and air fry for another 5 minutes. Cut the sandwich in half and enjoy!

## Greens Chips with Curried Yoghurt Sauce

**Prep time: 10 minutes | Cook time: 5 to 6 minutes | Serves 4**

| | |
|---|---|
| 240 ml low-fat Greek yoghurt | discarded, leaves cut into 2- to 3-inch pieces |
| 1 tablespoon freshly squeezed lemon juice | ½ bunch chard, stemmed, ribs removed and discarded, leaves cut into 2- to 3-inch pieces |
| 1 tablespoon curry powder | |
| ½ bunch curly kale, stemmed, ribs removed and | 1½ teaspoons olive oil |

Cook:
1. In a small bowl, stir together the yoghurt, lemon juice, and curry powder. Set aside.
2. In a large bowl, toss the kale and chard with the olive oil, working the oil into the leaves with your hands. This helps break up the fibres in the leaves so the chips are tender.
3. Air fry the greens in batches at 200ºC for 5 to 6 minutes, until crisp, shaking the drawer once during cooking.
4. Serve with the yoghurt sauce.

## Artichoke and Olive Pitta Flatbread & Stuffed Fried Mushrooms

**Prep time: 25 minutes | Cook time: 10 minutes | Serves 4-10**

**Artichoke and Olive Pitta Flatbread:**

| | |
|---|---|
| 2 wholewheat pitta bread | hearts, sliced |
| 2 tablespoons olive oil, divided | 70 g Kalamata olives |
| | 30 g shredded Parmesan |
| 2 garlic cloves, minced | 55 g crumbled feta cheese |
| ¼ teaspoon salt | Chopped fresh parsley, for garnish (optional) |
| 120 g canned artichoke | |

**Mushrooms:**

| | |
|---|---|
| 50 g panko breadcrumbs | 1 (227 g) package soft white cheese, at room temperature |
| ½ teaspoon freshly ground black pepper | 20 cremini or button mushrooms, stemmed |
| ½ teaspoon onion powder | |
| ½ teaspoon cayenne pepper | 1 to 2 tablespoons oil |

Prep for Artichoke and Olive Pitta Flatbread:
1. Brush each pitta with 1 tablespoon olive oil, then sprinkle the minced garlic and salt over the top. 3. Distribute the artichoke hearts, olives, and cheeses evenly between the two pitta bread, and place both into the Zone One of the air fryer.

Prep for Mushrooms:
1. In a medium-sized bowl, whisk the breadcrumbs, black pepper, onion powder, and cayenne until blended. 2. Add the soft white cheese and mix until well blended. Fill each mushroom top with 1 teaspoon of the soft white cheese mixture 3. Line the air fryer drawer in Zone Two with a piece of baking paper paper. 4. Place the mushrooms on the baking paper and spritz with oil.

Cook:
1. Set Zone One of the air fryer to 190ºC, select Bake, set the cook time to 10 minutes.
2. Press MATCH, set the temperature of Zone Two to 180ºC, set the cook time to 5 minutes.
3. Press Sync, then press START.
4. for Artichoke and Olive Pitta Flatbread, remove the pitta bread and cut them into 4 pieces each before serving. Sprinkle parsley over the top, if desired.
5. for the mushrooms, after cooking for 5 minutes, shake the drawer and cook for 5 to 6 minutes more until the filling is firm and the mushrooms are soft.

## Authentic Scotch Eggs

**Prep time: 15 minutes | Cook time: 11 to 13 minutes | Serves 6**

| | |
|---|---|
| 680 g bulk lean chicken or turkey sausage | divided |
| 3 raw eggs, divided | 65 g plain flour |
| 100 g dried breadcrumbs, | 6 hardboiled eggs, peeled |
| | Cooking oil spray |

Cook:
1. In a large bowl, combine the chicken sausage, 1 raw egg, and 40 g of breadcrumbs and mix well. Divide the mixture into 6 pieces and flatten each into a long oval.
2. In a shallow dish, beat the remaining 2 raw eggs.
3. Place the flour in a small bowl.
4. Place the remaining 80 g of breadcrumbs in a second small bowl.
5. Roll each hardboiled egg in the flour and wrap one of the chicken sausage pieces around each egg to encircle it completely.
6. One at a time, roll the encased eggs in the flour, dip in the beaten eggs, and finally dip in the breadcrumbs to coat.
7. Insert the crisper plate into the drawer and the drawer into the unit. Set the unit by selecting AIR FRY, setting the temperature to 190ºC, and setting the time to 3 minutes. Select START/STOP to begin.
8. Once the unit is set, spray the crisper plate with cooking oil. Place the eggs in a single layer into the drawer and spray them with oil.
9. Select AIR FRY, set the temperature to 190ºC, and set the time to 13 minutes. Select START/STOP to begin.
10. After about 6 minutes, use tongs to turn the eggs and spray them with more oil. Resume cooking for 5 to 7 minutes more, or until the chicken is thoroughly cooked and the Scotch eggs are browned.
11. When the cooking is complete, serve warm.

## Root Veggie Chips with Herb Salt

**Prep time: 10 minutes | Cook time: 8 minutes | Serves 2**

| | |
|---|---|
| 1 parsnip, washed | Cooking spray |
| 1 small beetroot, washed | Herb Salt: |
| 1 small turnip, washed | ¼ teaspoon rock salt |
| ½ small sweet potato, washed | 2 teaspoons finely chopped fresh parsley |
| 1 teaspoon olive oil | |

Cook:
1. Set the air fryer to 180ºC.
2. Peel and thinly slice the parsnip, beetroot, turnip, and sweet potato, then place the mixed vegetables in a large bowl, add the olive oil, and toss.
3. Spray the air fryer drawer with cooking spray, then place the mixed vegetables in the drawer and air fry for 8 minutes, gently shaking the drawer halfway through.
4. While the chips cook, make the herb salt in a small bowl by combining the rock salt and parsley.
5. Remove the chips and place on a serving plate, then sprinkle the herb salt on top and allow to cool for 2 to 3 minutes before serving.

## Parmesan Chips

**Prep time: 10 minutes | Cook time: 15 minutes per batch | Serves 2**

| | |
|---|---|
| 2 to 3 large russet potatoes or Maris Piper potatoes, peeled and cut into ½-inch sticks | ½ teaspoon salt |
| | Freshly ground black pepper, to taste |
| 2 teaspoons mixed vegetables or rapeseed oil | 1 teaspoon fresh chopped parsley |
| 50 g grated Parmesan cheese | |

Cook:
1. Bring a large saucepan of salted water to a boil on the hop while you peel and cut the potatoes. Blanch the potatoes in the boiling salted water for 4 minutes while you Set the air fryer to

52 | Chapter 7 Snacks and Appetizers

200°C. Strain the potatoes and rinse them with cold water. Dry them well with a clean kitchen towel.
2. Toss the dried potato sticks gently with the oil and place them in the air fryer drawer. Air fry for 25 minutes, shaking the drawer a few times while the fries cook to help them brown evenly.
3. Combine the Parmesan cheese, salt and pepper. With 2 minutes left on the air fryer cooking time, sprinkle the fries with the Parmesan cheese mixture. Toss the fries to coat them evenly with the cheese mixture and continue to air fry for the final 2 minutes, until the cheese has melted and just starts to brown. Sprinkle the finished fries with chopped parsley, a little more grated Parmesan cheese if you like, and serve.

## Crispy Cajun Fresh Dill Pickle Chips

**Prep time: 5 minutes | Cook time: 10 minutes | Makes 16 slices**

| | |
|---|---|
| 30 g plain flour | 2 large fresh dill pickled cucumbers, sliced into 8 rounds each |
| 42 g panko breadcrumbs | |
| 1 large egg, beaten | |
| 2 teaspoons Cajun seasoning | Cooking spray |

Cook:
1. Set the air fryer to 200°C.
2. Place the plain flour, panko breadcrumbs, and egg into 3 separate shallow dishes, then stir the Cajun seasoning into the flour.
3. Dredge each pickle chip in the flour mixture, then the egg, and finally the breadcrumbs. Shake off any excess, then place each coated pickle chip on a plate.
4. Spritz the air fryer drawer with cooking spray, then place 8 pickle chips in the drawer and air fry for 5 minutes, or until crispy and golden. Repeat this process with the remaining pickle chips.
5. Remove the chips and allow to slightly cool on a a wire rack before serving.

## Bacon-Wrapped Prawns and Jalapeño Chillies

**Prep time: 20 minutes | Cook time: 26 minutes | Serves 8**

| | |
|---|---|
| 24 large prawns, peeled and deveined, about 340 g | 12 strips bacon, cut in half |
| 5 tablespoons barbecue sauce, divided | 24 small pickled jalapeño chillies slices |

Cook:
1. Toss together the prawns and 3 tablespoons of the barbecue sauce. Let stand for 15 minutes. Soak 24 wooden cocktail sticks in water for 10 minutes. Wrap 1 piece bacon around the prawns and jalapeño chillies slice, then secure with a cocktail stick.
2. Set the air fryer to 180°C.
3. Working in batches, place half of the prawns in the air fryer drawer, spacing them ½ inch apart. Air fry for 10 minutes. Turn prawns over with tongs and air fry for 3 minutes more, or until bacon is golden and prawns are fully cooked.
4. Brush with the remaining barbecue sauce and serve.

# Chapter 8  Vegetables and Sides

## Marinara Pepperoni Mushroom Pizza

**Prep time: 5 minutes | Cook time: 18 minutes | Serves 4**

| | |
|---|---|
| 4 large portobello mushrooms, stems removed | 225 g shredded Mozzarella cheese |
| 4 teaspoons olive oil | 10 slices sugar-free pepperoni |
| 225 g marinara sauce | |

Cook:
1. Set the air fryer to 190ºC.
2. Brush each mushroom cap with the olive oil, one teaspoon for each cap.
3. Put on a baking sheet and bake, stem-side down, for 8 minutes.
4. Take out of the air fryer and divide the marinara sauce, Mozzarella cheese and pepperoni evenly among the caps.
5. Air fry for another 10 minutes until browned.
6. Serve hot.

## Roasted Radishes with Sea Salt

**Prep time: 5 minutes | Cook time: 18 minutes | Serves 4**

| | |
|---|---|
| 450 g radishes, ends trimmed if needed | 2 tablespoons olive oil |
| | ½ teaspoon sea salt |

Cook:
1. Set the air fryer to 180ºC.
2. In a large bowl, combine the radishes with olive oil and sea salt.
3. Pour the radishes into the air fryer and roast for 10 minutes. Stir or turn the radishes over and roast for 8 minutes more, then serve.

## Roasted Brussels Sprouts with Bacon

**Prep time: 10 minutes | Cook time: 20 minutes | Serves 4**

| | |
|---|---|
| 4 slices thick-cut bacon, chopped (about 110 g) | halved (or quartered if large) |
| 450 g Brussels sprouts, | Freshly ground black pepper, to taste |

Cook:
1. Set the air fryer to 190ºC.
2. Air fry the bacon for 5 minutes, shaking the drawer once or twice during the cooking time.
3. Add the Brussels sprouts to the drawer and drizzle a little bacon fat from the bottom of the air fryer drawer into the drawer. Toss the sprouts to coat with the bacon fat. Air fry for an additional 15 minutes, or until the Brussels sprouts are tender to a knifepoint.
4. Season with freshly ground black pepper.

## Asian-Inspired Roasted Broccoli

**Prep time: 10 minutes | Cook time: 15 minutes | Serves 4**

| | |
|---|---|
| Broccoli: | Sauce: |
| Oil, for spraying | 2 tablespoons soy sauce |
| 450 g broccoli florets | 2 teaspoons honey |
| 2 teaspoons peanut oil | 2 teaspoons Sriracha |
| 1 tablespoon minced garlic | 1 teaspoon rice vinegar |
| ½ teaspoon salt | |

Cook:
Make the Broccoli
1. Line the air fryer drawer with parchment and spray lightly with oil.
2. In a large bowl, toss together the broccoli, peanut oil, garlic, and salt until evenly coated.
3. Spread out the broccoli in an even layer in the prepared drawer.
4. Air fry at 200ºC for 15 minutes, stirring halfway through. Make the Sauce.
5. Meanwhile, in a small microwave-safe bowl, combine the soy sauce, honey, Sriracha, and rice vinegar and microwave on high for about 15 seconds. Stir to combine.
6. Transfer the broccoli to a serving bowl and add the sauce. Gently toss until evenly coated and serve immediately.

## Baked Jalapeño and Cheese Cauliflower Mash

**Prep time: 10 minutes | Cook time: 15 minutes | Serves 6**

| | |
|---|---|
| 1 (340 g) steamer bag cauliflower florets, cooked according to package instructions | 120 g shredded sharp Cheddar cheese |
| | 20 g pickled jalapeños |
| | ½ teaspoon salt |
| 2 tablespoons salted butter, softened | ¼ teaspoon ground black pepper |
| 60 g cream cheese, softened | |

Cook:
1. Place cooked cauliflower into a food processor with

remaining ingredients. Pulse twenty times until cauliflower is smooth and all ingredients are combined.
2. Spoon mash into an ungreased round nonstick baking dish. Place dish into air fryer drawer. Adjust the temperature to 190ºC and bake for 15 minutes. The top will be golden brown when done. Serve warm.

## Gorgonzola Mushrooms with Horseradish Mayo

**Prep time: 15 minutes | Cook time: 10 minutes | Serves 5**

| | |
|---|---|
| 60 g bread crumbs | stems removed |
| 2 cloves garlic, pressed | 55 g grated Gorgonzola cheese |
| 2 tablespoons chopped fresh coriander | 55 g low-fat mayonnaise |
| ⅓ teaspoon coarse sea salt | 1 teaspoon prepared horseradish, well-drained |
| ½ teaspoon crushed red pepper flakes | 1 tablespoon finely chopped fresh parsley |
| 1½ tablespoons olive oil | |
| 20 medium mushrooms, | |

Cook:
1. Set the air fryer to 190ºC.
2. Combine the bread crumbs together with the garlic, coriander, salt, red pepper, and olive oil.
3. Take equal-sized amounts of the bread crumb mixture and use them to stuff the mushroom caps. Add the grated Gorgonzola on top of each.
4. Put the mushrooms in a baking dish and transfer to the air fryer.
5. Air fry for 10 minutes, ensuring the stuffing is warm throughout.
6. In the meantime, prepare the horseradish mayo. Mix the mayonnaise, horseradish and parsley.
7. When the mushrooms are ready, serve with the mayo.

## Cauliflower Steaks Gratin

**Prep time: 10 minutes | Cook time: 13 minutes | Serves 2**

| | |
|---|---|
| 1 head cauliflower | thyme leaves |
| 1 tablespoon olive oil | 3 tablespoons grated Parmigiano-Reggiano cheese |
| Salt and freshly ground black pepper, to taste | 2 tablespoons panko bread crumbs |
| ½ teaspoon chopped fresh | |

Cook:
1. Set the air fryer to 190ºC.
2. Cut two steaks out of the centre of the cauliflower. To do this, cut the cauliflower in half and then cut one slice about 1-inch thick off each half. The rest of the cauliflower will fall apart into florets, which you can roast on their own or save for another meal.
3. Brush both sides of the cauliflower steaks with olive oil and season with salt, freshly ground black pepper and fresh thyme. Place the cauliflower steaks into the air fryer drawer and air fry for 6 minutes. Turn the steaks over and air fry for another 4 minutes. Combine the Parmesan cheese and panko bread crumbs and sprinkle the mixture over the tops of both steaks and air fry for another 3 minutes until the cheese has melted and the bread crumbs have browned.
4. Serve this with some sautéed bitter greens and air-fried blistered tomatoes.

## Broccoli-Cheddar Twice-Baked Potatoes

**Prep time: 10 minutes | Cook time: 46 minutes | Serves 4**

| | |
|---|---|
| Oil, for spraying | 1 tablespoon sour cream |
| 2 medium Maris Piper potatoes | 1 teaspoon garlic powder |
| 1 tablespoon olive oil | 1 teaspoon onion powder |
| 30 g broccoli florets | 60 g shredded Cheddar cheese |

Cook:
1. Line the air fryer drawer with parchment and spray lightly with oil.
2. Rinse the potatoes and pat dry with paper towels. Rub the outside of the potatoes with the olive oil and place them in the prepared drawer.
3. Air fry at 200ºC for 40 minutes, or until easily pierced with a fork. Let cool just enough to handle, then cut the potatoes in half lengthwise.
4. Meanwhile, place the broccoli in a microwave-safe bowl, cover with water, and microwave on high for 5 to 8 minutes. Drain and set aside.
5. Scoop out most of the potato flesh and transfer to a medium bowl.
6. Add the sour cream, garlic, and onion powder and stir until the potatoes are mashed.
7. Spoon the potato mixture back into the hollowed potato skins, mounding it to fit, if necessary. Top with the broccoli and cheese. Return the potatoes to the drawer. You may need to work in batches, depending on the size of your air fryer.
8. Air fry at 200ºC for 3 to 6 minutes, or until the cheese has melted.
9. Serve immediately.

## Blackened Courgette with Kimchi-Herb Sauce

**Prep time: 10 minutes | Cook time: 15 minutes | Serves 2**

| | |
|---|---|
| 2 medium courgettes, ends trimmed (about 170 g each) | garnish |
| 2 tablespoons olive oil | 2 tablespoons rice vinegar |
| 75 g kimchi, finely chopped | 2 teaspoons Asian chili-garlic sauce |
| 5 g finely chopped fresh coriander | 1 teaspoon grated fresh ginger |
| 5 g finely chopped fresh flat-leaf parsley, plus more for | coarse sea salt and freshly ground black pepper, to taste |

Cook:

1. Brush the courgettes with half of the olive oil, place in the air fryer, and air fry at 200°C, turning halfway through, until lightly charred on the outside and tender, about 15 minutes.
2. Meanwhile, in a small bowl, combine the remaining 1 tablespoon olive oil, the kimchi, coriander, parsley, vinegar, chili-garlic sauce, and ginger.
3. Once the courgette is finished cooking, transfer it to a colander and let it cool for 5 minutes. Using your fingers, pinch and break the courgette into bite-size pieces, letting them fall back into the colander. Season the courgette with salt and pepper, toss to combine, then let sit a further 5 minutes to allow some of its liquid to drain. Pile the courgette atop the kimchi sauce on a plate and sprinkle with more parsley to serve.

## Blistered Shishito Peppers with Lime Juice

**Prep time: 5 minutes | Cook time: 9 minutes | Serves 3**

| | |
|---|---|
| 230 g shishito peppers, rinsed | 1 tablespoon tamari or shoyu |
| Cooking spray | 2 teaspoons fresh lime juice |
| Sauce: | 2 large garlic cloves, minced |

Cook:

1. Set the air fryer to 200°C. Spritz the air fryer drawer with cooking spray.
2. Place the shishito peppers in the drawer and spritz them with cooking spray. Roast for 3 minutes.
3. Meanwhile, whisk together all the ingredients for the sauce in a large bowl. Set aside.
4. Shake the drawer and spritz them with cooking spray again, then roast for an additional 3 minutes.
5. Shake the drawer one more time and spray the peppers with cooking spray. Continue roasting for 3 minutes until the peppers are blistered and nicely browned.
6. Remove the peppers from the drawer to the bowl of sauce. Toss to coat well and serve immediately.

## Garlic Roasted Broccoli

**Prep time: 8 minutes | Cook time: 10 to 14 minutes | Serves 6**

| | |
|---|---|
| 1 head broccoli, cut into bite-size florets | Sea salt and freshly ground black pepper, to taste |
| 1 tablespoon avocado oil | 1 tablespoon freshly squeezed lemon juice |
| 2 teaspoons minced garlic | ½ teaspoon lemon zest |
| ⅛ teaspoon red pepper flakes | |

Cook:

1. In a large bowl, toss together the broccoli, avocado oil, garlic, red pepper flakes, salt, and pepper.
2. Set the air fryer to 190°C. Arrange the broccoli in a single layer in the air fryer drawer, working in batches if necessary. Roast for 10 to 14 minutes, until the broccoli is lightly charred.
3. Place the florets in a medium bowl and toss with the lemon juice and lemon zest. Serve.

## Broccoli with Sesame Dressing

**Prep time: 5 minutes | Cook time: 10 minutes | Serves 4**

| | |
|---|---|
| 425 g broccoli florets, cut into bite-size pieces | 2 tablespoons coconut aminos |
| 1 tablespoon olive oil | 2 tablespoons sesame oil |
| ¼ teaspoon salt | ½ teaspoon xylitol |
| 2 tablespoons sesame seeds | ¼ teaspoon red pepper flakes (optional) |
| 2 tablespoons rice vinegar | |

Cook:

1. Set the air fryer to 200°C.
2. In a large bowl, toss the broccoli with the olive oil and salt until thoroughly coated.
3. Transfer the broccoli to the air fryer drawer. Pausing halfway through the cooking time to shake the drawer, air fry for 10 minutes until the stems are tender and the edges are beginning to crisp.
4. Meanwhile, in the same large bowl, whisk together the sesame seeds, vinegar, coconut aminos, sesame oil, xylitol, and red pepper flakes (if using).
5. Transfer the broccoli to the bowl and toss until thoroughly coated with the seasonings.
6. Serve warm or at room temperature.

## Air Fried Potatoes with Olives

**Prep time: 15 minutes | Cook time: 40 minutes | Serves 1**

| | |
|---|---|
| 1 medium Maris Piper potatoes, scrubbed and peeled | ⅛ teaspoon salt |
| | Dollop of butter |
| | Dollop of cream cheese |
| 1 teaspoon olive oil | 1 tablespoon Kalamata olives |
| ¼ teaspoon onion powder | 1 tablespoon chopped chives |

Cook:
1. Set the air fryer to 200ºC.
2. In a bowl, coat the potatoes with the onion powder, salt, olive oil, and butter.
3. Transfer to the air fryer and air fry for 40 minutes, turning the potatoes over at the halfway point.
4. Take care when removing the potatoes from the air fryer and serve with the cream cheese, Kalamata olives and chives on top.

## Lemon-Thyme Asparagus

**Prep time: 5 minutes | Cook time: 4 to 8 minutes | Serves 4**

| | |
|---|---|
| 450 g asparagus, woody ends trimmed off | Sea salt and freshly ground black pepper, to taste |
| 1 tablespoon avocado oil | 60 g goat cheese, crumbled |
| ½ teaspoon dried thyme or ½ tablespoon chopped fresh thyme | Zest and juice of 1 lemon |
| | Flaky sea salt, for serving (optional) |

Cook:
1. In a medium bowl, toss together the asparagus, avocado oil, and thyme, and season with sea salt and pepper.
2. Place the asparagus in the air fryer drawer in a single layer. Set the air fryer to 200ºC and air fry for 4 to 8 minutes, to your desired doneness.
3. Transfer to a serving platter. Top with the goat cheese, lemon zest, and lemon juice. If desired, season with a pinch of flaky salt.

## Tamarind Sweet Potatoes

**Prep time: 5 minutes | Cook time: 20 to 25 minutes | Serves 4**

| | |
|---|---|
| 5 garnet sweet potatoes, peeled and diced | juice |
| | 1 tablespoon butter, melted |
| 1½ tablespoons fresh lime | 2 teaspoons tamarind paste |
| 1½ teaspoon ground allspice | ½ teaspoon turmeric powder |
| ⅓ teaspoon white pepper | A few drops liquid stevia |

Cook:
1. Set the air fryer to 200ºC.
2. In a large mixing bowl, combine all the ingredients and toss until the sweet potatoes are evenly coated.
3. Place the sweet potatoes in the air fryer drawer and air fry for 20 t0 25 minutes, or until the potatoes are crispy on the outside and soft on the inside. Shake the drawer twice during cooking.
4. Let the potatoes cool for 5 minutes before serving.

## Spinach and Sweet Pepper Poppers

**Prep time: 10 minutes | Cook time: 8 minutes | Makes 16 poppers**

| | |
|---|---|
| 110 g cream cheese, softened | 8 mini sweet bell peppers, tops removed, seeded, and halved lengthwise |
| 20 g chopped fresh spinach leaves | |
| ½ teaspoon garlic powder | |

Cook:
1. In a medium bowl, mix cream cheese, spinach, and garlic powder. Place 1 tablespoon mixture into each sweet pepper half and press down to smooth.
2. Place poppers into ungreased air fryer drawer. Adjust the temperature to 200ºC and air fry for 8 minutes. Poppers will be done when cheese is browned on top and peppers are tender-crisp.
3. Serve warm.

## Courgette Balls

**Prep time: 5 minutes | Cook time: 10 minutes | Serves 4**

| | |
|---|---|
| 4 courgettes | 1 tablespoon Italian herbs |
| 1 egg | 75 g grated coconut |
| 45 g grated Parmesan cheese | |

Cook:
1. Thinly grate the courgettes and dry with a cheesecloth, ensuring to remove all the moisture.
2. In a bowl, combine the courgettes with the egg, Parmesan, Italian herbs, and grated coconut, mixing well to incorporate everything. Using the hands, mold the mixture into balls.
3. Set the air fryer to 200ºC.
4. Lay the courgette balls in the air fryer drawer and air fry for 10 minutes.
5. Serve hot.

## Tahini-Lemon Kale

**Prep time: 5 minutes | Cook time: 15 minutes | Serves 2 to 4**

| | |
|---|---|
| 60 g tahini | 110 g packed torn kale leaves (stems and ribs removed and leaves torn into palm-size pieces) |
| 60 g fresh lemon juice | |
| 2 tablespoons olive oil | |
| 1 teaspoon sesame seeds | |
| ½ teaspoon garlic powder | coarse sea salt and freshly ground black pepper, to taste |
| ¼ teaspoon cayenne pepper | |

Cook:

1. In a large bowl, whisk together the tahini, lemon juice, olive oil, sesame seeds, garlic powder, and cayenne until smooth. Add the kale leaves, season with salt and black pepper, and toss in the dressing until completely coated. Transfer the kale leaves to a cake pan.
2. Place the pan in the air fryer and roast at 180°C, stirring every 5 minutes, until the kale is wilted and the top is lightly browned, about 15 minutes. Remove the pan from the air fryer and serve warm.

## Sausage-Stuffed Mushroom Caps

**Prep time: 10 minutes | Cook time: 8 minutes | Serves 2**

| | |
|---|---|
| 6 large portobello mushroom caps | finely ground almond flour |
| 230 g Italian sausage | 20 g grated Parmesan cheese |
| 15 g chopped onion | 1 teaspoon minced fresh garlic |
| 2 tablespoons blanched | |

Cook:

1. Use a spoon to hollow out each mushroom cap, reserving scrapings.
2. In a medium skillet over medium heat, brown the sausage about 10 minutes or until fully cooked and no pink remains. Drain and then add reserved mushroom scrapings, onion, almond flour, Parmesan, and garlic. Gently fold ingredients together and continue cooking an additional minute, then remove from heat.
3. Evenly spoon the mixture into mushroom caps and place the caps into a 6-inch round pan. Place pan into the air fryer drawer.
4. Adjust the temperature to 190°C and set the timer for 8 minutes.
5. When finished cooking, the tops will be browned and bubbling.
6. Serve warm.

## Glazed Carrots

**Prep time: 10 minutes | Cook time: 8 to 10 minutes | Serves 4**

| | |
|---|---|
| 2 teaspoons honey | ⅛ teaspoon ginger |
| 1 teaspoon orange juice | 450 g baby carrots |
| ½ teaspoon grated orange rind | 2 teaspoons olive oil |
| | ¼ teaspoon salt |

Cook:

1. Combine honey, orange juice, grated rind, and ginger in a small bowl and set aside.
2. Toss the carrots, oil, and salt together to coat well and pour them into the air fryer drawer.
3. Roast at 200°C for 5 minutes. Shake drawer to stir a little and cook for 2 to 4 minutes more, until carrots are barely tender.
4. Pour carrots into a baking dish.
5. Stir the honey mixture to combine well, pour glaze over carrots, and stir to coat.
6. Roast at 180°C for 1 minute or just until heated through.

## Easy Greek Briami (Ratatouille)

**Prep time: 15 minutes | Cook time: 40 minutes | Serves 6**

| | |
|---|---|
| 2 Maris Piper potatoes, cubed | 1 teaspoon dried parsley |
| | 1 teaspoon dried oregano |
| 100 g plum tomatoes, cubed | ½ teaspoon salt |
| 1 aubergine, cubed | ½ teaspoon black pepper |
| 1 courgette, cubed | ¼ teaspoon red pepper flakes |
| 1 red onion, chopped | 80 ml olive oil |
| 1 red pepper, chopped | 1 (230 g) can tomato paste |
| 2 garlic cloves, minced | 65 ml vegetable stock |
| 1 teaspoon dried mint | 65 ml water |

Cook:

1. Set the air fryer to 160°C.
2. In a large bowl, combine the potatoes, tomatoes, aubergine, courgette onion, bell pepper, garlic, mint, parsley, oregano, salt, black pepper, and red pepper flakes.
3. In a small bowl, mix together the olive oil, tomato paste, stock, and water.
4. Pour the oil-and-tomato-paste mixture over the vegetables and toss until everything is coated.
5. Pour the coated vegetables into the air fryer drawer in an even layer and roast for 20 minutes. After 20 minutes, stir well and spread out again. Roast for an additional 10 minutes, then repeat the process and cook for another 10 minutes.

## Indian Aubergine Bharta

**Prep time: 15 minutes | Cook time: 20 minutes | Serves 4**

| | |
|---|---|
| 1 medium aubergine | juice |
| 2 tablespoons vegetable oil | 2 tablespoons chopped fresh coriander |
| 25 g finely minced onion | ½ teaspoon coarse sea salt |
| 100 g finely chopped fresh tomato | ⅛ teaspoon cayenne pepper |
| 2 tablespoons fresh lemon | |

Cook:

1. Rub the aubergine all over with the vegetable oil. Place the aubergine in the air fryer drawer. Set the air fryer to 200°C for 20 minutes, or until the aubergine skin is blistered and charred.
2. Transfer the aubergine to a re-sealable plastic bag, seal, and set aside for 15 to 20 minutes (the aubergine will finish cooking in the residual heat trapped in the bag).
3. Transfer the aubergine to a large bowl. Peel off and discard the charred skin. Roughly mash the aubergine flesh. Add the onion, tomato, lemon juice, coriander, salt, and cayenne. Stir to combine.

## Corn Croquettes

**Prep time: 10 minutes | Cook time: 12 to 14 minutes | Serves 4**

| | |
|---|---|
| 105 g leftover mashed potatoes | pepper |
| 340 g corn kernels (if frozen, thawed, and well drained) | ¼ teaspoon salt |
| | 50 g panko bread crumbs |
| ¼ teaspoon onion powder | Oil for misting or cooking spray |
| ⅛ teaspoon ground black | |

Cook:

1. Place the potatoes and half the corn in food processor and pulse until corn is well chopped.
2. Transfer mixture to large bowl and stir in remaining corn, onion powder, pepper and salt.
3. Shape mixture into 16 balls.
4. Roll balls in panko crumbs, mist with oil or cooking spray, and place in air fryer drawer.
5. Air fry at 180°C for 12 to 14 minutes, until golden brown and crispy.

## Southwestern Roasted Corn

**Prep time: 10 minutes | Cook time: 10 minutes | Serves 4**

**Corn:**

| | |
|---|---|
| 240 g thawed frozen corn kernels | 1 tablespoon fresh lemon juice |
| 50 g diced yellow onion | 1 teaspoon ground cumin |
| 150 g mixed diced bell peppers | ½ teaspoon ancho chili powder |
| 1 jalapeño, diced | ½ teaspoon coarse sea salt |

**for Serving:**

| | |
|---|---|
| 150 g queso fresco or feta cheese | 1 tablespoon fresh lemon juice |
| 10 g chopped fresh coriander | |

Cook:

1. for the corn: In a large bowl, stir together the corn, onion, bell peppers, jalapeño, lemon juice, cumin, chili powder, and salt until well incorporated.
2. Pour the spiced vegetables into the air fryer drawer. Set the air fryer to 190°C for 10 minutes, stirring halfway through the cooking time.
3. Transfer the corn mixture to a serving bowl. Add the cheese, coriander, and lemon juice and stir well to combine.
4. Serve immediately.

## Easy Rosemary Green Beans

**Prep time: 5 minutes | Cook time: 5 minutes | Serves 1**

| | |
|---|---|
| 1 tablespoon butter, melted | 3 cloves garlic, minced |
| 2 tablespoons rosemary | 95 g chopped green beans |
| ½ teaspoon salt | |

Cook:

1. Set the air fryer to 200°C.
2. Combine the melted butter with the rosemary, salt, and minced garlic. Toss in the green beans, coating them well.
3. Air fry for 5 minutes.
4. Serve immediately.

## Roasted Brussels Sprouts with Orange and Garlic

**Prep time: 5 minutes | Cook time: 10 minutes | Serves 4**

- 450 g Brussels sprouts, quartered
- 2 garlic cloves, minced
- 2 tablespoons olive oil
- ½ teaspoon salt
- 1 orange, cut into rings

Cook:
1. Set the air fryer to 180°C.
2. In a large bowl, toss the quartered Brussels sprouts with the garlic, olive oil, and salt until well coated.
3. Pour the Brussels sprouts into the air fryer, lay the orange slices on top of them, and roast for 10 minutes.
4. Remove from the air fryer and set the orange slices aside. Toss the Brussels sprouts before serving.

# Chapter 9    Vegetarian Mains

## Lush Vegetables Roast

**Prep time: 15 minutes | Cook time: 20 minutes | Serves 6**

| | |
|---|---|
| 315 g small parsnips, peeled and cubed | cubed |
| 315 g celery | 1 tablespoon fresh thyme needles |
| 2 red onions, sliced | 1 tablespoon olive oil |
| 315 g small butternut squash, cut in half, deseeded and | Salt and ground black pepper, to taste |

Cook:

1. Set the air fryer to 200°C.
2. Combine the cut vegetables with the thyme, olive oil, salt and pepper.
3. Put the vegetables in the drawer and transfer the drawer to the air fryer.
4. Roast for 20 minutes, stirring once throughout the roasting time, until the vegetables are nicely browned and cooked through.
5. Serve warm.

## Spinach-Artichoke Stuffed Mushrooms

**Prep time: 10 minutes | Cook time: 10 to 14 minutes | Serves 4**

| | |
|---|---|
| 2 tablespoons olive oil | 120 g chopped marinated artichoke hearts |
| 4 large portobello mushrooms, stems removed and gills scraped out | 235 g frozen spinach, thawed and squeezed dry |
| ½ teaspoon salt | 120 g grated Parmesan cheese |
| ¼ teaspoon freshly ground pepper | 2 tablespoons chopped fresh parsley |
| 110 g goat cheese, crumbled | |

Cook:

1. Set the air fryer to 200°C.
2. Rub the olive oil over the portobello mushrooms until thoroughly coated.
3. Sprinkle both sides with the salt and black pepper.
4. Place top-side down on a clean work surface.
5. In a small bowl, combine the goat cheese, artichoke hearts, and spinach.
6. Mash with the back of a fork until thoroughly combined.
7. Divide the cheese mixture among the mushrooms and sprinkle with the Parmesan cheese.
8. Air fry for 10 to 14 minutes until the mushrooms are tender and the cheese has begun to brown.
9. Top with the fresh parsley just before serving.

## Mediterranean Air Fried Veggies

**Prep time: 10 minutes | Cook time: 6 minutes | Serves 4**

| | |
|---|---|
| 1 large courgette, sliced | 1 teaspoon mixed herbs |
| 235 g cherry tomatoes, halved | 1 teaspoon mustard |
| 1 parsnip, sliced | 1 teaspoon garlic purée |
| 1 green pepper, sliced | 6 tablespoons olive oil |
| 1 carrot, sliced | Salt and ground black pepper, to taste |

Cook:

1. Set the air fryer to 200°C.
2. Combine all the ingredients in a bowl, making sure to coat the vegetables well.
3. Transfer to the air fryer and air fry for 6 minutes, ensuring the vegetables are tender and browned.
4. Serve immediately.

## Pesto Vegetable Skewers

**Prep time: 30 minutes | Cook time: 8 minutes | Makes 8 skewers**

| | |
|---|---|
| 1 medium courgette, trimmed and cut into ½-inch slices | 16 whole cremini or chestnut mushrooms |
| ½ medium brown onion, peeled and cut into 1-inch squares | 80 ml basil pesto |
| | ½ teaspoon salt |
| 1 medium red pepper, seeded and cut into 1-inch squares | ¼ teaspoon ground black pepper |

Cook:

1. Divide courgette slices, onion, and pepper into eight even portions.
2. Place on 6-inch skewers for a total of eight kebabs.
3. Add 2 mushrooms to each skewer and brush kebabs generously with pesto.
4. Sprinkle each kebab with salt and black pepper on all sides, then place into ungreased air fryer drawer.
5. Adjust the temperature to 190°C and air fry for 8 minutes, turning kebabs halfway through cooking.
6. Vegetables will be browned at the edges and tender-crisp when done.
7. Serve warm.

## Cheesy Cabbage Wedges

**Prep time: 5 minutes | Cook time: 20 minutes | Serves 4**

| | |
|---|---|
| 4 tablespoons melted butter | Salt and black pepper, to taste |
| 1 head cabbage, cut into wedges | 120 g shredded Mozzarella cheese |
| 235 g shredded Parmesan cheese | |

Cook:
1. Set the air fryer to 190°C.
2. Brush the melted butter over the cut sides of cabbage wedges and sprinkle both sides with the Parmesan cheese.
3. Season with salt and pepper to taste.
4. Place the cabbage wedges in the air fryer drawer and air fry for 20 minutes, flipping the cabbage halfway through, or until the cabbage wedges are lightly browned.
5. Transfer the cabbage wedges to a plate and serve with the Mozzarella cheese sprinkled on top.

## Courgette-Ricotta Tart

**Prep time: 15 minutes | Cook time: 60 minutes | Serves 6**

| | |
|---|---|
| 120 g grated Parmesan cheese, divided | 1 courgette, thinly sliced (about 475 ml) |
| 350 g almond flour | 235 g Ricotta cheese |
| 1 tablespoon coconut flour | 3 eggs |
| ½ teaspoon garlic powder | 2 tablespoons double cream |
| ¾ teaspoon salt, divided | 2 cloves garlic, minced |
| 60 g unsalted butter, melted | ½ teaspoon dried tarragon |

Cook:
1. Set the air fryer to 170°C.
2. Coat a round pan with olive oil and set aside.
3. In a large bowl, whisk 60 g Parmesan with the almond flour, coconut flour, garlic powder, and ¼ teaspoon of the salt.
4. Stir in the melted butter until the dough resembles coarse crumbs.
5. Press the dough firmly into the bottom and up the sides of the prepared pan.
6. Air fry for 12 to 15 minutes until the crust begins to brown.
7. Let cool to room temperature.
8. Meanwhile, place the courgette in a colander and sprinkle with the remaining ½ teaspoon salt.
9. Toss gently to distribute the salt and let sit for 30 minutes.
10. Use paper towels to pat the courgette dry.
11. In a large bowl, whisk together the ricotta, eggs, double cream, garlic, and tarragon.
12. Gently stir in the courgette slices.
13. Pour the cheese mixture into the cooled crust and sprinkle with the remaining 60 g Parmesan.
14. Increase the air fryer to 180°C.
15. Place the pan in the air fryer drawer and air fry for 45 to 50 minutes, or until set and a tester inserted into the centre of the tart comes out clean.
16. Serve warm or at room temperature.

## Air Fryer Winter Vegetables

**Prep time: 5 minutes | Cook time: 16 minutes | Serves 2**

| | |
|---|---|
| 1 parsnip, sliced | 1 tablespoon chopped fresh thyme |
| 235 g sliced butternut squash | 2 teaspoons olive oil |
| 1 small red onion, cut into wedges | Salt and black pepper, to taste |
| ½ chopped celery stalk | |

Cook:
1. Set the air fryer to 190°C.
2. Toss all the ingredients in a large bowl until the vegetables are well coated.
3. Transfer the vegetables to the air fryer drawer and air fry for 16 minutes, shaking the drawer halfway through, or until the vegetables are golden brown and tender.
4. Remove from the drawer and serve warm.

## Roasted Vegetables with Rice

**Prep time: 5 minutes | Cook time: 12 minutes | Serves 4**

| | |
|---|---|
| 2 teaspoons melted butter | 1 garlic clove, minced |
| 235 g chopped mushrooms | Salt and black pepper, to taste |
| 235 g cooked rice | 2 hard-boiled eggs, grated |
| 235 g peas | 1 tablespoon soy sauce |
| 1 carrot, chopped | |
| 1 red onion, chopped | |

Cook:
1. Set the air fryer to 190°C.
2. Coat a baking dish with melted butter.
3. Stir together the mushrooms, cooked rice, peas, carrot, onion, garlic, salt, and pepper in a large bowl until well mixed.
4. Pour the mixture into the prepared baking dish and transfer to the air fryer drawer.
5. Roast in the set air fryer for 12 minutes until the vegetables

are tender.
6. Divide the mixture among four plates.
7. Serve warm with a sprinkle of grated eggs and a drizzle of soy sauce.

## Courgette and Spinach Croquettes

**Prep time: 9 minutes | Cook time: 7 minutes | Serves 6**

| | |
|---|---|
| 4 eggs, slightly beaten | 120 g Parmesan cheese, grated |
| 120 g almond flour | ⅓ teaspoon red pepper flakes |
| 120 g goat cheese, crumbled | 450 g courgette, peeled and grated |
| 1 teaspoon fine sea salt | |
| 4 garlic cloves, minced | ⅓ teaspoon dried dill weed |
| 235 g baby spinach | |

Cook:
1. Thoroughly combine all ingredients in a bowl.
2. Now, roll the mixture to form small croquettes.
3. Air fry at 170°C for 7 minutes or until golden.
4. Tate, adjust for seasonings and serve warm.

## Spinach Cheese Casserole

**Prep time: 15 minutes | Cook time: 15 minutes | Serves 4**

| | |
|---|---|
| 1 tablespoon salted butter, melted | 60 g chopped pickled jalapeños |
| 60 g diced brown onion | 475 g fresh spinach, chopped |
| 227 g full fat soft white cheese | 475 g cauliflower florets, chopped |
| 80 g full-fat mayonnaise | 235 g artichoke hearts, chopped |
| 80 g full-fat sour cream | |

Cook:
1. In a large bowl, mix butter, onion, soft white cheese, mayonnaise, and sour cream.
2. Fold in jalapeños, spinach, cauliflower, and artichokes.
3. Pour the mixture into a round baking dish.
4. Cover with foil and place into the air fryer drawer.
5. Adjust the temperature to 190°C and set the timer for 15 minutes.
6. In the last 2 minutes of cooking, remove the foil to brown the top.
7. Serve warm.

# Chapter 10　Desserts

## Gingerbread

**Prep time: 5 minutes | Cook time: 20 minutes | Makes 1 loaf**

| | |
|---|---|
| Cooking spray | ⅛ teaspoon salt |
| 65 g All-purpose flour | 1 egg |
| 2 tablespoons granulated sugar | 70 g treacle |
| | 120 ml buttermilk |
| ¾ teaspoon ground ginger | 2 tablespoons coconut, or avocado oil |
| ¼ teaspoon cinnamon | |
| 1 teaspoon baking powder | 1 teaspoon pure vanilla extract |
| ½ teaspoon baking soda | |

Cook:

1. Set the air fryer to 160°C.
2. Spray a baking dish lightly with cooking spray.
3. In a medium bowl, mix together all the dry ingredients.
4. In a separate bowl, beat the egg. Add treacle, buttermilk, oil, and vanilla and stir until well mixed.
5. Pour liquid mixture into dry ingredients and stir until well blended.
6. Pour batter into baking dish and bake for 20 minutes, or until toothpick inserted in center of loaf comes out clean.

## Air Fryer Apple Fritters

**Prep time: 30 minutes | Cook time: 7 to 8 minutes | Serves 6**

| | |
|---|---|
| 1 chopped, peeled Granny Smith apple | 1 teaspoon salt |
| | 2 tablespoons milk |
| 90 g granulated sugar | 2 tablespoons butter, melted |
| 1 teaspoon ground cinnamon | 1 large egg, beaten |
| 60 g All-purpose flour | Cooking spray |
| 1 teaspoon baking powder | 15 g icing sugar (optional) |

Cook:

1. Mix together the apple, granulated sugar, and cinnamon in a small bowl. Allow to sit for 30 minutes.
2. Combine the flour, baking powder, and salt in a medium bowl. Add the milk, butter, and egg and stir to incorporate.
3. Pour the apple mixture into the bowl of flour mixture and stir with a spatula until a dough forms.
4. Make the fritters: On a clean work surface, divide the dough into 12 equal portions and shape into 1-inch balls. Flatten them into patties with your hands.
5. Set the air fryer to 180°C. Line the air fryer drawer with baking paper and spray it with cooking spray.
6. Transfer the apple fritters onto the baking paper, evenly spaced but not too close together. Spray the fritters with cooking spray.
7. Bake for 7 to 8 minutes until lightly browned. Flip the fritters halfway through the cooking time.
8. Remove from the drawer to a plate and serve with the confectioners' sugar sprinkled on top, if desired.

## Strawberry Shortcake

**Prep time: 10 minutes | Cook time: 25 minutes | Serves 6**

| | |
|---|---|
| 2 tablespoons coconut oil | 1 teaspoon baking powder |
| 55g blanched finely ground almond flour | 1 teaspoon vanilla extract |
| | 240 g heavy cream, whipped |
| 2 large eggs, whisked | 6 medium fresh strawberries, hulled and sliced |
| 100 g granulated sweetener | |

Cook:

1. In a large bowl, combine coconut oil, flour, eggs, sweetener, baking powder, and vanilla. Pour batter into an ungreased round nonstick baking dish.
2. Place dish into air fryer drawer. Adjust the temperature to 150°C and bake for 25 minutes. When done, shortcake should be golden, and a toothpick inserted in the middle will come out clean.
3. Remove dish from fryer and let cool 1 hour.
4. Once cooled, top cake with whipped cream and strawberries to serve.

## Vanilla Pound Cake

**Prep time: 10 minutes | Cook time: 25 minutes | Serves 6**

| | |
|---|---|
| 55 g blanched finely ground almond flour | 1 teaspoon baking powder |
| | 120 ml full-fat sour cream |
| 55 g salted butter, melted | 30 g full-fat cream cheese, softened |
| 100 g granulated sweetener | |
| 1 teaspoon vanilla extract | 2 large eggs |

Cook:

1. In a large bowl, mix almond flour, butter, and sweetener.
2. Add in vanilla, baking powder, sour cream, and cream cheese and mix until well combined. Add eggs and mix.
3. Pour batter into a round baking dish. Place pan into the air fryer drawer.
4. Adjust the temperature to 150°C and bake for 25 minutes.
5. When the cake is done, a toothpick inserted in center will come out clean. The center should not feel wet. Allow it to cool completely, or the cake will crumble when moved.

## Lime Bars

**Prep time: 10 minutes | Cook time: 33 minutes | Makes 12 bars**

| 140 g blanched finely ground almond flour, divided | 4 tablespoons salted butter, melted |
| --- | --- |
| 40 g powdered sweetener, divided | 120 ml fresh lime juice |
| | 2 large eggs, whisked |

Cook:

1. In a medium bowl, mix together 110 g flour, 25 g sweetener, and butter. Press mixture into bottom of an ungreased round nonstick cake pan.
2. Place pan into air fryer drawer. Adjust the temperature to 150ºC and bake for 13 minutes. Crust will be brown and set in the middle when done.
3. Allow to cool in pan 10 minutes.
4. In a medium bowl, combine remaining flour, remaining sweetener, lime juice, and eggs. Pour mixture over cooled crust and return to air fryer for 20 minutes. Top will be browned and firm when done.
5. Let cool completely in pan, about 30 minutes, then chill covered in the refrigerator 1 hour.
6. Serve chilled.

## Rhubarb and Strawberry Crumble

**Prep time: 10 minutes | Cook time: 12 to 17 minutes | Serves 6**

| 250 g sliced fresh strawberries | flour, or All-purpose flour |
| --- | --- |
| 95 g sliced rhubarb | 40 g packed light brown sugar |
| 40 g granulated sugar | ½ teaspoon ground cinnamon |
| 30 g quick-cooking oatmeal | 3 tablespoons unsalted butter, melted |
| 25 g whole-wheat pastry | |

Cook:

1. Insert the crisper plate into the drawer and the drawer into the unit. Set the unit to 190ºC.
2. In a 6-by-2-inch round metal baking dish, combine the strawberries, rhubarb, and granulated sugar.
3. In a medium bowl, stir together the oatmeal, flour, brown sugar, and cinnamon. Stir the melted butter into this mixture until crumbly. Sprinkle the crumble mixture over the fruit.
4. Once the unit is set, place the pan into the drawer.
5. Bake for 12 minutes then check the crumble. If the fruit is bubbling and the topping is golden brown, it is done. If not, resume cooking.
6. When the cooking is complete, serve warm.

## Protein Powder Doughnut Holes

**Prep time: 25 minutes | Cook time: 6 minutes | Makes 12 holes**

| 25g blanched finely ground almond flour | ½ teaspoon baking powder |
| --- | --- |
| 30 g low-carb vanilla protein powder | 1 large egg |
| | 5 tablespoons unsalted butter, melted |
| 100 g granulated sweetener | ½ teaspoon vanilla extract |

Cook:

1. Mix all ingredients in a large bowl. Place into the freezer for 20 minutes.
2. Wet your hands with water and roll the dough into twelve balls.
3. Cut a piece of baking paper to fit your air fryer drawer. Working in batches as necessary, place doughnut holes into the air fryer drawer on top of baking paper.
4. Adjust the temperature to 190ºC and air fry for 6 minutes.
5. Flip doughnut holes halfway through the cooking time.
6. Let cool completely before serving.

## Biscuit-Base Cheesecake

**Prep time: 10 minutes | Cook time: 20 minutes | Serves 8**

| 100 g crushed digestive biscuits | 35 g granulated sugar |
| --- | --- |
| 3 tablespoons butter, at room temperature | 2 eggs, beaten |
| | 1 tablespoon all-purpose flour |
| 225 g cream cheese, at room temperature | 1 teaspoon vanilla extract |
| | 60 ml chocolate syrup |

Cook:

1. In a small bowl, stir together the crushed biscuits and butter. Press the crust into the bottom of a 6-by-2-inch round baking dish and freeze to set while you prepare the filling.
2. In a medium bowl, stir together the cream cheese and sugar until mixed well.
3. One at a time, beat in the eggs. Add the flour and vanilla and stir to combine.
4. Transfer ⅓ of the filling to a small bowl and stir in the chocolate syrup until combined.
5. Insert the crisper plate into the drawer and the drawer into the unit. Set the air fryer to 160ºC, and bake for 3 minutes.
6. Pour the vanilla filling into the pan with the crust. Drop the chocolate filling over the vanilla filling by the spoonful. With a clean butter knife stir the fillings in a zigzag pattern to marble them. Do not let the knife touch the crust.
7. Once the unit is set, place the pan into the drawer.

8. Set the temperature to 160ºC, and bake for 20 minutes.
9. When the cooking is done, the cheesecake should be just set. Cool on a wire rack for 1 hour. Refrigerate the cheesecake until firm before slicing.

## Kentucky Chocolate Nut Pie

### Prep time: 20 minutes | Cook time: 25 minutes | Serves 8

| | |
|---|---|
| 2 large eggs, beaten | pecans |
| 75 g unsalted butter, melted | 170 g milk chocolate chips |
| 160 g granulated sugar | 2 tablespoons bourbon, or peach juice |
| 30 g All-purpose flour | |
| 190 g coarsely chopped | 1 (9-inch) unbaked piecrust |

### Cook:

1. In a large bowl, stir together the eggs and melted butter. Add the sugar and flour and stir until combined. Stir in the pecans, chocolate chips, and bourbon until well mixed.
2. Using a fork, prick holes in the bottom and sides of the pie crust. Pour the pie filling into the crust.
3. Set the air fryer to 180ºC.
4. Cook for 25 minutes, or until a knife inserted into the middle of the pie comes out clean.
5. Let set for 5 minutes before serving.

## Boston Cream Donut Holes

### Prep time: 30 minutes | Cook time: 4 minutes per batch | Makes 24 donut holes

| | |
|---|---|
| 100 g bread flour | butter, melted |
| 1 teaspoon active dry yeast | Vegetable oil |
| 1 tablespoon granulated sugar | Custard Filling: |
| | 95 g box French vanilla instant pudding mix |
| ¼ teaspoon salt | |
| 120 ml warm milk | 175 ml whole milk |
| ½ teaspoon pure vanilla extract | 60 ml heavy cream |
| | Chocolate Glaze: |
| 2 egg yolks | 170 g chocolate chips |
| 2 tablespoons unsalted | 80 ml heavy cream |

### Cook:

1. Combine the flour, yeast, sugar, and salt in the bowl of a stand mixer. Add the milk, vanilla, egg yolks and butter. Mix until the dough starts to come together in a ball. Transfer the dough to a floured surface and knead the dough by hand for 2 minutes. Shape the dough into a ball, place it in a large, oiled bowl, cover the bowl with a clean kitchen towel and let the dough rise for 1 to 1½ hours or until the dough has doubled in size.
2. When the dough has risen, punch it down and roll it into a 24-inch log. Cut the dough into 24 pieces and roll each piece into a ball. Place the dough balls on a baking sheet and let them rise for another 30 minutes.
3. Set the air fryer to 200ºC.
4. Spray or brush the dough balls lightly with vegetable oil and air fry eight at a time for 4 minutes, turning them over halfway through the cooking time.
5. While donut holes are cooking, make the filling and chocolate glaze. Make the filling: Use an electric hand mixer to beat the French vanilla pudding, milk and ¼ cup of heavy cream together for 2 minutes.
6. Make the chocolate glaze: Place the chocolate chips in a medium-sized bowl. Bring the heavy cream to a boil on the stovetop and pour it over the chocolate chips. Stir until the chips are melted and the glaze is smooth.
7. To fill the donut holes, place the custard filling in a pastry bag with a long tip. Poke a hole into the side of the donut hole with a small knife. Wiggle the knife around to make room for the filling. Place the pastry bag tip into the hole and slowly squeeze the custard into the center of the donut. Dip the top half of the donut into the chocolate glaze, letting any excess glaze drip back into the bowl. Let the glazed donut holes sit for a few minutes before serving.

## Vanilla and Cardamon Walnuts Tart

### Prep time: 5 minutes | Cook time: 13 minutes | Serves 6

| | |
|---|---|
| 240 ml coconut milk | 2 eggs |
| 60 g walnuts, ground | 1 teaspoon vanilla essence |
| 30 g powdered sweetener | ¼ teaspoon ground cardamom |
| 30 g almond flour | |
| 55 g butter, at room temperature | ¼ teaspoon ground cloves |
| | Cooking spray |

### Cook:

1. Set the air fryer to 180ºC. Coat a baking dish with cooking spray.
2. Combine all the ingredients except the oil in a large bowl and stir until well blended. Spoon the batter mixture into the baking dish.
3. Bake in the set air fryer for approximately 13 minutes. Check the tart for doneness: If a toothpick inserted into the center of the tart comes out clean, it's done.
4. Remove from the air fryer and place on a wire rack to cool. Serve immediately.

## Crustless Peanut Butter Cheesecake

**Prep time: 10 minutes | Cook time: 10 minutes | Serves 2**

| | |
|---|---|
| 110 g cream cheese, softened | sugar-added peanut butter |
| 2 tablespoons powdered sweetener | ½ teaspoon vanilla extract |
| 1 tablespoon all-natural, no- | 1 large egg, whisked |

Cook:
1. In a medium bowl, mix cream cheese and sweetener until smooth. Add peanut butter and vanilla, mixing until smooth. Add egg and stir just until combined.
2. Spoon mixture into an ungreased springform pan and place into air fryer drawer. Adjust the temperature to 150°C and bake for 10 minutes. Edges will be firm, but center will be mostly set with only a small amount of jiggle when done.
3. Let pan cool at room temperature 30 minutes, cover with plastic wrap, then place into refrigerator at least 2 hours.
4. Serve chilled.

## Lush Chocolate Chip Cookies

**Prep time: 7 minutes | Cook time: 9 minutes | Serves 4**

| | |
|---|---|
| 3 tablespoons butter, at room temperature | chocolate |
| 50 g light brown sugar, plus 1 tablespoon | ¼ teaspoon baking soda |
| 1 egg yolk | ½ teaspoon vanilla extract |
| 35 g All-purpose flour | 120 g semisweet chocolate chips |
| 2 tablespoons ground white | Nonstick flour-infused baking spray |

Cook:
1. In medium bowl, beat together the butter and brown sugar until fluffy. Stir in the egg yolk.
2. Add the flour, white chocolate, baking soda, and vanilla and mix well. Stir in the chocolate chips.
3. Line a 6-by-2-inch round baking dish with baking paper. Spray the baking paper with flour-infused baking spray.
4. Insert the crisper plate into the drawer and the drawer into the unit. Set the unit to 150°C.
5. Spread the batter into the prepared pan, leaving a ½-inch border on all sides.
6. Once the unit is set, place the pan into the drawer.
7. Bake to cookies for 9 minutes.
8. When the cooking is complete, the cookies should be light brown and just barely set. Remove the pan from the drawer and let cool for 10 minutes. Remove the cookie from the pan, remove the baking paper, and let cool completely on a wire rack.

## Breaded Bananas with Chocolate Topping

**Prep time: 10 minutes | Cook time: 10 minutes | Serves 6**

| | |
|---|---|
| 20 g cornflour | 3 bananas, halved crosswise |
| 25 g plain breadcrumbs | Cooking spray |
| 1 large egg, beaten | Chocolate sauce, for serving |

Cook:
1. Set the air fryer to 180°C.
2. Place the cornflour, breadcrumbs, and egg in three separate bowls.
3. Roll the bananas in the cornstarch, then in the beaten egg, and finally in the breadcrumbs to coat well.
4. Spritz the air fryer drawer with the cooking spray. 5. Arrange the banana halves in the drawer and mist them with the cooking spray. Air fry for 5 minutes. Flip the bananas and continue to air fry for another 2 minutes. 6. Remove the bananas from the drawer to a serving plate. Serve with the chocolate sauce drizzled over the top.

## Peanut Butter, Honey & Banana Toast

**Prep time: 10 minutes | Cook time: 9 minutes | Serves 4**

| | |
|---|---|
| 2 tablespoons unsalted butter, softened | 2 bananas, peeled and thinly sliced |
| 4 slices white bread | 4 tablespoons honey |
| 4 tablespoons peanut butter | 1 teaspoon ground cinnamon |

Cook:
1. Spread butter on one side of each slice of bread, then peanut butter on the other side. Arrange the banana slices on top of the peanut butter sides of each slice (about 9 slices per toast). Drizzle honey on top of the banana and sprinkle with cinnamon.
2. Cut each slice in half lengthwise so that it will better fit into the air fryer drawer. Arrange two pieces of bread, butter sides down, in the air fryer drawer. Set the air fryer to 190°C cooking for 5 minutes. Then set the air fryer to 200°C and cook for an additional 4 minutes, or until the bananas have started to brown. Repeat with remaining slices.
3. Serve hot.

# Appendix : Recipe Index

## A

Air Fried Crispy Venison · 34
Air Fried Potatoes with Olives · 58
Air Fried Tortilla Chips & Spinach and Carrot Balls · 19
Air Fryer Apple Fritters · 67
Air Fryer Fish Fry · 41
Air Fryer Winter Vegetables · 64
Almond Pesto Salmon · 43
Artichoke and Olive Pitta Flatbread & Stuffed Fried Mushrooms · 51
Asian-Inspired Roasted Broccoli · 55
Asparagus and Bell Pepper Strata · 5
Authentic Scotch Eggs · 52

## B

Bacon-Wrapped Prawns and Jalapeño Chillies · 53
Bacon-Wrapped Scallops · 39
Baked Jalapeño and Cheese Cauliflower Mash · 55
Bang Bang Prawns · 43
Beef Jerky · 14
Beery and Crunchy Onion Rings · 18
Beetroot Salad with Lemon Vinaigrette · 17
Beignets & Churro Bites · 14
Biscuit-Base Cheesecake · 68
Blackened Cajun Chicken Tenders · 27
Blackened Courgette with Kimchi-Herb Sauce · 57
Blackened Red Snapper · 43
Blistered Shishito Peppers with Lime Juice · 57
BLT Breakfast Wrap & Meritage Eggs · 10
Blue Cheese Steak Salad · 31
Boston Cream Donut Holes · 69
Breaded Bananas with Chocolate Topping · 70
Breakfast Sausage and Cauliflower & Vanilla Granola · 11
Broccoli and Cheese Stuffed Chicken · 28
Broccoli with Sesame Dressing · 57
Broccoli-Cheddar Twice-Baked Potatoes · 56
Bulgogi Burgers · 35
Butter and Bacon Chicken · 28
Buttery Sweet Potatoes · 19

## C

Carrot Chips · 47
Cauliflower Avocado Toast & Drop Biscuits · 8
Cauliflower Steaks Gratin · 56
Celery Chicken & Spicy Chicken Thighs and Gold Potatoes 26
Cheesy Cabbage Wedges · 64
Cheesy Chilli Toast · 20
Cheesy Potato Patties · 17
Chicken Drumsticks with Barbecue-Honey Sauce · 26
Chicken Hand Pies · 23
Chicken Patties · 23
Chicken Schnitzel Dogs · 28
Chilli Tilapia · 42
Cinnamon Rolls & Ham and Cheese Crescents · 7
Cod with Avocado · 41
Corn Croquettes · 60
Courgette and Spinach Croquettes · 65
Courgette Balls · 58
Courgette-Ricotta Tart · 64
Crab and Bell Pepper Cakes · 42
Crab Cakes · 44
Crispy Cajun Fresh Dill Pickle Chips · 53
Crunchy Basil White Beans · 49
Crunchy Chicken with Roasted Carrots · 22
Crustless Peanut Butter Cheesecake · 70
Dark Chocolate and Cranberry Granola Bars · 49

## D

Dukkah-Crusted Halibut · 44

## E

Easy Greek Briami (Ratatouille) · 59

Easy Rosemary Green Beans ··········· 60
Easy Turkey Tenderloin ··········· 22

## F

Filo Vegetable Triangles & Old Bay Tilapia ··········· 13
Fish Croquettes with Lemon-Dill Aioli ··········· 40
Five-Spice Pork Belly ··········· 34
French Garlic Chicken ··········· 25
Friday Night Fish-Fry ··········· 45
Fried Catfish Fillets ··········· 44
Fried Catfish with Dijon Sauce ··········· 41

## G

Garlic Butter Steak Bites ··········· 36
Garlic Edamame ··········· 47
Garlic Roasted Broccoli ··········· 57
Gingerbread ··········· 67
Glazed Carrots ··········· 59
Goat Cheese-Stuffed Bavette Steak ··········· 36
Golden Avocado Tempura & Italian Egg Cups ··········· 6
Golden Prawns ··········· 39
Gorgonzola Mushrooms with Horseradish Mayo ··········· 56
Greens Chips with Curried Yoghurt Sauce ··········· 51
Grilled Ham and Cheese on Raisin Bread ··········· 51

## H

Herb-Buttermilk Chicken Breast ··········· 24
Herb-Roasted Beef Tips with Onions ··········· 35
Herb-Roasted Veggies ··········· 18
Herbed Lamb Steaks ··········· 33
Honey-Mustard Chicken Wings ··········· 49
Hush Puppies ··········· 47

## I

Indian Aubergine Bharta ··········· 60
Indian-Style Sweet Potato Fries ··········· 17
Italian Flavour Chicken Breasts with Roma Tomatoes ······· 26
Italian Rice Balls ··········· 48
Italian Sausages with Peppers and Onions ··········· 34

## K

Kentucky Chocolate Nut Pie ··········· 69

Keto Quiche ··········· 9

## L

Lemon-Pepper Chicken Chicken Drumsticks ··········· 50
Lemon-Thyme Asparagus ··········· 58
Lime Bars ··········· 68
Lush Chocolate Chip Cookies ··········· 70
Lush Vegetables Roast ··········· 63

## M

Marinara Pepperoni Mushroom Pizza ··········· 55
Mediterranean Air Fried Veggies ··········· 63
Mexican-Style Shredded Beef ··········· 37
Mississippi Spice Muffins & Cheddar-Ham-Corn Muffins ·· 10
Mixed Berry Crumble & Scallops with Green Vegetables ···· 13
Mushroom in Bacon-Wrapped Filets Mignons ··········· 36
Mustard Herb Pork Tenderloin ··········· 37
Mustard Lamb Chops ··········· 32
Mustard-Crusted Fish Fillets ··········· 45

## N

Nashville Hot Chicken ··········· 27
Nutty Granola ··········· 9

## O

One-Dish Chicken and Rice ··········· 25
Onion Omelette & Spinach Omelet ··········· 8
Orange-Mustard Glazed Salmon ··········· 42

## P

Paprika Crab Burgers ··········· 39
Parmesan Chips ··········· 52
Parmesan-Crusted Hake with Garlic Sauce ··········· 43
Peanut Butter Chicken Satay ··········· 22
Peanut Butter, Honey & Banana Toast ··········· 70
Pepper Steak ··········· 32
Peppered Maple Bacon Knots & Smoky Sausage Patties ····· 7
Pesto Vegetable Skewers ··········· 63
Pork Burgers with Red Cabbage Salad & Berry Cheesecake 14
Pork Kebab with Yogurt Sauce & Beef Mince Taco Rolls ··· 33
Pork Loin Roast ··········· 33
Pork Rind Fried Chicken ··········· 27

72 | Appendix : Recipe Index

| | |
|---|---|
| Pork Shoulder with Garlicky Coriander-Parsley Sauce | 32 |
| Potato-Crusted Chicken | 29 |
| Potatoes Lyonnaise | 5 |
| Poutine with Waffle Fries | 47 |
| Prawns Egg Rolls | 48 |
| Prawns with Smoky Tomato Dressing | 40 |
| Protein Powder Doughnut Holes | 68 |
| Purple Potato Chips with Rosemary | 18 |

## R

| | |
|---|---|
| Red Pepper Tapenade | 51 |
| Rhubarb and Strawberry Crumble | 68 |
| Roasted Brussels Sprouts with Bacon | 55 |
| Roasted Brussels Sprouts with Orange and Garlic | 61 |
| Roasted Grape Dip | 50 |
| Roasted Radishes with Sea Salt | 55 |
| Roasted Vegetables with Rice | 64 |
| Root Veggie Chips with Herb Salt | 52 |
| Rosemary and Orange Roasted Chickpeas | 18 |

## S

| | |
|---|---|
| Sausage and Pork Meatballs | 36 |
| Sausage Balls with Cheese | 50 |
| Sausage Stuffed Peppers & Bacon Eggs on the Go | 5 |
| Sausage-Stuffed Mushroom Caps | 59 |
| Scalloped Veggie Mix | 17 |
| Scallops and Spinach with Cream Sauce | 42 |
| Simple and Easy Croutons & Bacon Pinwheels | 19 |
| Sirloin Steaks with Eggs | 8 |
| Snapper Scampi | 41 |
| Sole and Asparagus Bundles | 39 |
| Southwestern Roasted Corn | 60 |
| Spice-Rubbed Pork Loin | 31 |

| | |
|---|---|
| Spice-Rubbed Turkey Breast | 22 |
| Spinach and Crab Meat Cups | 48 |
| Spinach and Sweet Pepper Poppers | 58 |
| Spinach Cheese Casserole | 65 |
| Spinach-Artichoke Stuffed Mushrooms | 63 |
| Steak with Bell Pepper | 35 |
| Steak, Broccoli, and Mushroom Rice Bowls | 31 |
| Steamed Tuna with Lemongrass | 40 |
| Strawberry Shortcake | 67 |
| String Bean Fries | 50 |
| Super Easy Bacon Cups & Southwestern Ham Egg Cups | 6 |

## T

| | |
|---|---|
| Tahini-Lemon Kale | 59 |
| Tamarind Sweet Potatoes | 58 |
| Teriyaki Chicken Legs | 24 |
| Thai Tacos with Peanut Sauce | 25 |
| Tuna Cakes | 40 |
| Turkish Chicken Kebabs | 23 |
| Tuscan Air Fried Veal Loin | 37 |

## V

| | |
|---|---|
| Vanilla and Cardamon Walnuts Tart | 69 |
| Vanilla Pound Cake | 67 |
| Veggie Salmon Nachos | 49 |
| Vietnamese Grilled Pork | 31 |

## Y

| | |
|---|---|
| Yakitori & Crisp Paprika Chicken Drumsticks | 24 |

## Z

| | |
|---|---|
| Zesty London Broil | 37 |

Printed in Great Britain
by Amazon